Family Background and University Success

Family Background and University Success

Differences in Higher Education Access and Outcomes in England

Claire Crawford
Lorraine Dearden
John Micklewright
Anna Vignoles

OXFORD
UNIVERSITY PRESS

OXFORD
UNIVERSITY PRESS

Great Clarendon Street, Oxford, OX2 6DP,
United Kingdom

Oxford University Press is a department of the University of Oxford.
It furthers the University's objective of excellence in research, scholarship,
and education by publishing worldwide. Oxford is a registered trade mark of
Oxford University Press in the UK and in certain other countries

First Edition published in 2017
Impression: 1

Published in the United States of America by Oxford University Press
198 Madison Avenue, New York, NY 10016, United States of America

British Library Cataloguing in Publication Data
Data available

Library of Congress Control Number: 2016940972

ISBN 978–0–19–968913–2

Printed in Great Britain by
Clays Ltd, St Ives plc

Acknowledgements

This book stems from a project funded by the Nuffield Foundation, 'Higher Education Funding and Access: Exploring Common Beliefs'. We are very grateful to the Foundation for supporting our research, and especially to the Director for Education, Josh Hillman, for his encouragement, his patience, and his comments. We also thank our project steering group for their valuable input at different stages of the work: Nick Barr (chair), Gavan Conlon, Robin Naylor, the late David Raffe, and Charles Ritchie. Their assistance included very useful comments on a draft of the first chapter of this book and on our plans for other chapters. We would like to thank Paul Johnson for his invaluable comments on a complete first draft. Helpful comments on parts of the manuscript were also made by Tony Atkinson and Tina Gericke.

Other financial support for the research was received from the Economic and Social Research Council, The British Academy, the Department for Business, Innovation and Skills, the Department for Education, the Sutton Trust, Universities UK, and UCL Institute of Education.

Two colleagues worked closely with us on the project and we would like to acknowledge their important contributions to its success: Jake Anders (UCL Institute of Education) and Wenchao Jin (Institute for Fiscal Studies). Other colleagues who have co-authored papers that we draw on include Emla Fitzsimons, Alissa Goodman, John Jerrim, Lindsey Macmillan and Gill Wyness (UCL Institute of Education), Jack Britton, Rowena Crawford and Laura van der Erve (Institute for Fiscal Studies), and Haroon Chowdry (Early Intervention Foundation).

The views expressed in the book are our own and should not be associated with any of the institutions with which we are affiliated or with our funders.

London
April 2016

Table of Contents

List of Figures

List of Tables

List of Tables

1

Family Background and University Success—What are the Issues?

In 1900 the son of a relief railway station master in rural Leicestershire, the grandfather of one of the authors, was admitted as an undergraduate to the University of Oxford. It is hard now to imagine quite how rare entry to any university would have been for someone from his background. Rarer still had his father been a labourer or even a clerk—and almost unheard of had he been one of his three sisters. Schooling to any age had only been compulsory in England for twenty years. The year before, 1899, had seen the minimum school leaving age raised to just twelve.

Roll forward a hundred years. Past the legislation at the end of the Second World War providing free secondary schools. Past the landmark Robbins Report of 1963, with its principle that higher education 'should be available for all those who are qualified by ability and attainment'. Past the subsequent creation of polytechnics and their transformation into universities in the early 1990s. As in other rich industrialized countries, an enormously expanded university system has emerged as the demand for graduates has risen in line with changes in the structure of market economies.[1] In 1900, just over one per cent of each age cohort entered full-time higher education and barely 25,000 students at all stages were enrolled—going to university was in fact unusual for people of all origins. The figures rose only slowly in the next fifty years. But by

---

[1] The history of higher education in England is documented in Gillard, D. (2011), *Education in England: a brief history*, http://www.educationengland.org.uk/history. The famous quotation from Robbins is from Chapter 2 paragraph 32: The Robbins Report (1963) *Higher Education. Report of the Committee appointed by the Prime Minister under the Chairmanship of Lord Robbins*. London: HMSO. The figures for total student numbers in 1900 and 2010 that follow come from the Robbins Report, Table 3, and the Higher Education Statistics Agency website (students not domiciled in the UK have not been included).

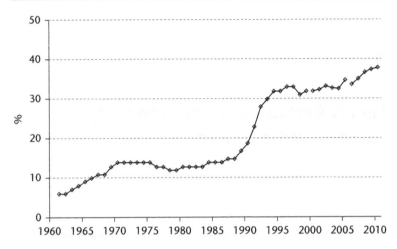

Figure 1.1. Young people entering higher education (%), 1961–2010

Notes: 1961–99: number of persons living in the UK aged under 21 years who are initial entrants to full-time and sandwich undergraduate courses of higher education in Britain as a percentage of the averaged 18 to 19-year-old British population. 2000–10: higher education participation rate (HEIPR) for 17–20-year-olds resident in England (figures for 2000–5 estimated by adjusting the HEPIR for 17–29-year-olds by the average ratio for 2006–10 of the rate for 17–20-year-olds to the rate for 17–29-year-olds).

Sources: 1961–99: Elias, P. and Purcell, K. (2004), *The Earnings of Graduates in Their Early Careers*, Warwick Institute for Employment Research, Figure 1; 2000–10: Department for Business, Education and Skills (2014), *Participation Rates in Higher Education: Academic Years 2006/2007–2012/2013 (Provisional)*, 24 August, Tables 1, A and B.

the start of the twenty-first century, after several different phases of post-war growth, about a third of young people entered higher education by their twenties—see Figure 1.1—the result of increases in both the supply of university places and the demand for them. By 2010, there were over two million undergraduate and postgraduate students in total. Universities have long ceased to be the preserve of a small privileged minority. And more women now go to university than men, reversing the inequality between the sexes of a century earlier.

But large differences in entry to university by family background remain—by level of income, by parental education, and by other measures of material and social advantage. The huge expansion in higher education certainly benefited people from all backgrounds. The child of the modern equivalent of a relief railway station master is now vastly more likely to go to university than a hundred years ago. The increase in the chances of university entry has been even greater for the son or daughter of a road mender or a cleaner. However, children from these

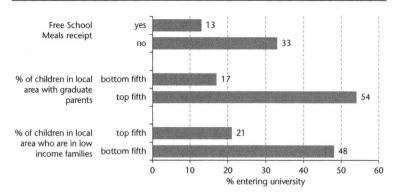

Figure 1.2. University participation rates (%), by family background, 2005/6

Notes: The figures for participation by Free School Meals receipt refer to the UK. The figures based on the two local area indicators refer to England and show the percentage of 18–19-year-olds who enter university in two groups of local areas, those in the bottom and top fifths of the distribution of all local areas ranked on the indicator concerned.

Sources: Department of Business, Industry and Skills (2012), *Widening Participation in Higher Education*, Table 1 (Free School Meals); Higher Education Funding Council for England (2010), *Trends in Young Participation in Higher Education: core results for England*, January 2010/03, Figures 19 and 23 (estimates from line graphs).

backgrounds are nowhere near as likely to go to university as the child of a doctor, a lawyer, or a senior company executive. The teenager of poor parents is much less likely to enter higher education than the offspring of a rich family. Large gaps in university entrance between children from different backgrounds are an enduring feature of British higher education, and indeed of many other countries' systems.

Figure 1.2 illustrates the magnitude of these gaps. The graph shows the percentage of young people who go to university—the 'university participation' rate. The data are all for 2005/6. They come from a time *before* the controversial increases in university tuition fees in much of the UK that took place in the following year and then again in 2012/13. They provide a baseline from which to assess the changes in university entry among young people from different backgrounds that have occurred alongside the substantial increases in fees. The gap in the percentage going to university between teenagers who received Free School Meals, a state benefit for families on low incomes, and other teenagers shows a striking difference. Not much more than one in ten (13 per cent) of those who were eligible for free meals went to university in 2005/6, compared to a third (33 per cent) of those who were not.

Put another way, teenagers from families not receiving free meals were two and a half times more likely to go to university than their peers in low-income families who qualified for this benefit.

These differences are much cited, but they have the disadvantage of being based on data that lump together the great majority of teenagers who do not get free meals—about six in every seven pupils in state schools. The other two measures in the graph allow for more gradation in family background, at the cost of moving to indicators that refer not to individual characteristics, but to those of the local area where a young person's family lives. (The data in these cases refer to England only.) 54 per cent of young people living in the top fifth of areas ranked by the proportion of parents with a degree were in higher education in 2005/6, a figure over three times higher than the 17 per cent for young people living in the bottom fifth of areas. The gaps are almost as striking across local areas ranked by the percentage of families receiving low-income state benefits: 48 per cent of young people in higher education are in the bottom fifth of areas—those with the lowest rates of benefit receipt—compared with 21 per cent in the top fifth of areas with families with the highest rates of benefit receipt.

Since 2005/6, policy on funding higher education in England has shifted considerably, however. The jump in the maximum tuition fee in October 2012, from less than £3,500 per year to £9,000 per year, has been the cause of particular concern. These fee increases, which we describe in more detail in Chapter 3, are centre stage in our analysis in this book. Governments everywhere in the industrialized world have had to decide how to finance greatly expanded provision of higher education. Various approaches have been adopted and we will see that the approach taken in England has been different to that of many countries. Many people fear that the sharply higher fees threaten the chances of young people from poorer backgrounds and even from middle-income families of entering higher education. In Chapter 4 we show that, on the whole, these concerns do not appear to have been realized.

The data in Figure 1.2 refer to entry to *any* university. But the one hundred and fifty or so universities in the UK are not all the same. They vary greatly in status. This reflects a range of factors including age, size, research intensity, the prior academic achievement of their students, and, as we will see later, the wages earned by their graduates. The ranking of universities has become much more salient in recent years, with a proliferation of league tables produced by newspapers and other organizations. Besides the differences by family background in the likelihood of going to any university, there are also marked differences

Table 1.1. Entry to any university and to 'high status' universities (%), top and bottom fifths of socio-economic status: 18 and 19-year-olds in England in 2005/6

	% who enter any university	% of all entrants who go to a 'high status' university
Top fifth (most advantaged)	52.0	41.7
Bottom fifth (least advantaged)	12.0	18.5

Notes: Young people who took their GCSEs in England aged 16 in 2001/2, with university entry in either 2004/5 or 2005/6 anywhere in the UK. The 41 universities defined as 'high status' are listed in Chowdry, H., Crawford, C., Dearden, L., Goodman, A., and Vignoles, A. (2013), 'Widening participation in higher education: analysis using linked administrative data', *Journal of the Royal Statistical Society*, Series A, 176: 431–57, Table 2).

Source: Authors' calculations based on administrative data linking all pupils attending schools in England to all students attending universities in the UK.

in the chances of entry to 'high status' institutions, however these are defined.

Press reports sometimes draw attention to the tiny numbers of teenagers receiving free school meals who enter Oxford and Cambridge, universities that are among the most prestigious and selective institutions. The high share of 'Oxbridge' undergraduates who come from private schools, around 45 per cent in 2010, is also the subject of frequent comment.[2] But the issue of entry to elite institutions goes well beyond just these two universities. There are sharp differences by family background in entry to a much broader group of high status institutions. The data in Table 1.1, like those used earlier, again pre-date the rise in university fees in 2006/7. About forty institutions are defined as 'high status' in this analysis, made up of the 'Russell Group' of leading universities, which include Oxford and Cambridge, together with other universities that have performed well in official ratings of university research. Around one third of young full-time university entrants attend one of these institutions.

The first column of figures shows the percentage of young people attending state schools in England who went on to enter any university in the UK, irrespective of its status, immediately after school or with a delay of a year. These data re-enforce the message of Figure 1.2. We distinguish between teenagers from the top and bottom fifths of the distribution of an index of socio-economic background. The index combines information on receipt of free school meals and the characteristics of the area in which each pupil lived at the end of secondary school

---

[2] The Oxbridge intake and its changes over time are well described in Bolton, P. (2014), *Oxbridge 'Elitism'*, House of Commons Library Standard Note SN/SG/616, 9 June.

(of the type used in Figure 1.2 but with a more extensive list of indicators). Just over half of teenagers from the most advantaged family backgrounds go to university but only one in eight of those from the least advantaged backgrounds—the bottom fifth of the socio-economic distribution. Put in betting terms, the odds of going to university are about evens with the advantaged family but 7 to 1 against with the disadvantaged one.

The second column focuses on just those teenagers managing to enter university. Among those who do go on to higher education, around 40 per cent of teenagers from the most advantaged family backgrounds enter one of the high status universities. But only about a fifth of those from the least advantaged families who get to university enter a high status institution: about four-fifths of them enter other, lower status, universities. Clearly young people from less advantaged backgrounds are much less likely to go to university at all. And if they do go, it is much less likely to be to a high status institution.

Up to this point, we have referred only to entry to higher education, to getting to university at all. This topic occupies a large part of our book. But the 'university success' of the book's title covers more than succeeding in a university application and taking up the place that is offered. We are also concerned with success while at university—and beyond, following graduation. Success means avoiding the risk of dropping out from university and thus completing the course of study. It means doing well in university exams and other forms of assessment and hence getting a good final degree mark—a good degree 'class' as it is called in the UK. And it means making the most of the degree obtained, in the sense of getting a good job after graduating or, in some cases, of going on to postgraduate study. These aspects of university success have received less attention in the literature than has entry to university. But they are also covered in our book because the evidence shows that here too there are clear differences in outcomes by family background.

For example, data on students entering one of the UK's older universities—those established prior to 1992—in 1989 enable us to assess how likely are students whose parents work in different occupations to drop out of university before completing their degrees. Figure 1.3 classifies male students into seven groups on the basis of their parents' social class, and shows that just over 8 per cent of those from the highest social class backgrounds dropped out of university before completing their degree, compared to almost 19 per cent of those whose parents are unemployed. The probability of dropping out is therefore more than twice as high for students whose parents did not have a job than for students whose parents worked in a professional occupation.

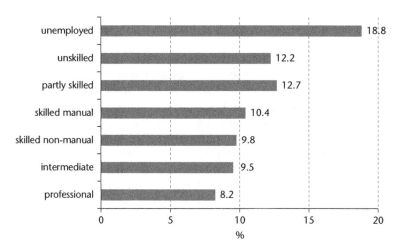

Figure 1.3. Male university entrants dropping out before completing their degree (%), by parents' social class, 1989/90

Notes: The population of interest covers male students who entered university in 1989/90 and left (either dropped out or graduated) by 1992/3. Students are classified as having dropped out if they withdraw from their course at any time between entering and starting the second term of their third year of study.

Source: Smith, J. and Naylor, R. (2001), 'Dropping out of university: a statistical analysis of the probability of withdrawal for UK university students', *Journal of the Royal Statistical Society*, Series A, 164: 389–405.

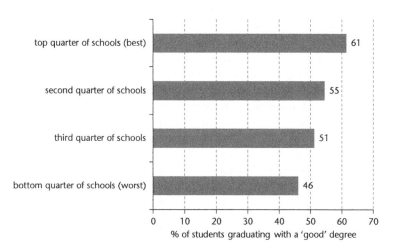

Figure 1.4. University entrants graduating with a 'good' degree (%), by performance of school attended prior to entry, 1997/8

Note: The population of interest covers students entering university full-time to study for a first degree at age 18 in 1997/8 or age 19 in 1998/9. A 'good' degree is defined as one where the student has been awarded one of the two highest degree classes available in the UK (out of five). Pupils are grouped on the basis of the average A-level point score per entry of the school they attended prior to entering university.

Source: Hefce (2005), 'Schooling effects on higher education achievement: further analysis— entry at 19', Higher Education Funding Council for England Issues Paper 2005/9.

There are also differences in how likely students from different backgrounds are to leave university with a 'good' degree (by which we mean one of the two highest degree classes in the UK—a first or an upper second class degree). Figure 1.4 uses data on 18- and 19-year-olds who entered higher education in the late 1990s and groups these students according to the performance of the school they attended before going to university. It shows that while 61 per cent of university entrants who went to one of the schools in the top quarter before going on to higher education graduated with a 'good' degree, just 46 per cent of university entrants from one of the bottom quarter of schools did the same, a gap of 15 percentage points.

Why do the Family Background Gaps Matter?

There are clearly substantial differences in a whole range of measures of university success by family background. But it is not enough to state that there are large gaps for young people from different family backgrounds in the chances of going to university, in the types of university that they go to, and in other aspects of university success—and then just to analyse those gaps. We must first explain why the gaps matter.

They matter for two reasons. First, higher education is one key route through which young people can secure better employment and earnings prospects. A half of all adults in England now apparently believe that getting a degree does not represent good value for money.[3] But all the evidence shows that there is a strong 'rate of return' to university degrees. It is often said that a degree is worth more than £100,000, net of tax, over a working life. Or, measured in another way, a standard three-year undergraduate degree programme in the UK has been estimated to increase earnings by 27 per cent compared to possession of two or more 'A' levels, academic qualifications taken by around half of all students at the end of 'further' education (the non-compulsory education level between school and university).[4] These large wage returns have

---

[3] Ormston, R. and Paterson, L. (2015), 'Higher Education', in Ormston, R. and Curtice, J. (eds), *British Social Attitudes: the 32nd Report*, London: NatCen Social Research. The extent to which this scepticism holds for those young people and their parents at the margin of actually making a decision on going to university is unknown.

[4] This estimate comes from Department of Business, Innovation and Skills (2011), 'The Returns to Higher Education Qualifications', BIS Research Paper 45. People citing the £100,000 figure include the former Minister for Universities and Science, David Willetts (http://blogs.channel4.com/factcheck/do-graduates-earn-100000-more-than-non-graduates).

persisted despite the major expansion in higher education that has occurred in recent decades. Demand for high-skill labour has remained strong, which appears to have sustained the premium for graduate wages. And there are many other benefits to the individual from higher education too—the 2012 Milburn Report on higher education and social mobility summarized these by arguing that graduates are 'healthier and happier', as well as 'wealthier'.[5]

Of course, the benefits from higher education—better earnings and improvements in other aspects of living standards—will vary from graduate to graduate. The estimate of £100,000 for earnings is just an average: some people will get considerably more than a 27 per cent addition to their earnings as a result of their degree and some considerably less. One dimension of the variation in the return to higher education is the university attended. The returns tend to be greater for degrees from 'high status' universities. They also tend to be greater for degrees in certain subjects (such as economics and medicine) and for those who are awarded higher degree classes.[6] Recent evidence strongly suggests that at least part of this variation reflects a genuine causal impact. That is, graduates from the best universities earn more because they have been to those universities and not because of any higher ability or other attribute that got them to a high status institution in the first place, for example. One reason for this may be that major employers tend to focus their graduate recruitment efforts on a small subset of universities and on graduates with only the two highest degree classes.[7]

---

[5] The Milburn Report (2012), *University Challenge: How Higher Education Can Advance Social Mobility: A progress report by the Independent Reviewer on Social Mobility and Child Poverty*, The Cabinet Office.

[6] Higher returns from higher status universities in the UK are documented in Chevalier, A. (2014), 'Does Higher Education Quality Matter in the UK?' in Polachek, S. and Tatsiramos, K. (eds), *Factors Affecting Worker Well-being: The Impact of Change in the Labor Market (Research in Labor Economics, Volume 40)*, Emerald Group Publishing Limited. Higher returns for certain subjects are documented in Walker, I. and Zhu, Y. (2011), 'Differences by degree: Evidence of the net financial rates of return to undergraduate studies for England and Wales', *Economics of Education Review*, 30: 1177–86. Recent evidence on the variation in graduate earnings by subject and institution is offered by Britton, J., Dearden, L., Shephard, N. and Vignoles, A. (2016), 'How English domiciled graduate earnings vary with gender, institution, subject and socio economic background', IFS Working Paper W16/06, London: Institute for Fiscal Studies. Higher returns for higher degree classes are documented in Feng, A. and Graetz, G. (2013), 'A question of degree: the effects of degree class on labour market outcomes', *Centre for Economic Performance Discussion Paper 1221*, London School of Economics, London, UK.

[7] The Milburn Report cites evidence of the concentration of top employers' graduate recruitment efforts on a small minority of universities. Many employers look for graduates with a first or upper second class (2:1) degree. Around half of graduates in the UK are awarded these degree classes; see Chapter 7 for more details.

These benefits for the individual mean that gaps by family background in university entry—including those in entry to different status universities—and degree completion translate into substantial differences in earnings and other aspects of living standards. The first source of concern over such gaps is therefore based on considerations of fairness or equity. The cycle of social and economic disadvantage that exists across the generations can be broken, or at least reduced, if able young people from poorer backgrounds can go to university, finish their degrees, and then pass on the benefits of doing so to their own children. In short, higher education can potentially help sever the link between childhood poverty and poor prospects in adulthood.[8]

The second reason is based on considerations of economic efficiency. Talent may be wasted and the economy therefore suffer if able young people from more disadvantaged backgrounds are not succeeding in higher education—in entering the system, in going to the best universities, and in completing their degrees. This is not to argue that university is the only worthwhile route for a talented young person. But, undeniably, it is one important route. The UK's competitiveness in the global economy depends on maximizing its use of resources, especially in high-skill industries. The university system has a major role to play in this, drawing in as many persons as possible who have the ability to benefit from what higher education has to offer. Indeed, the government announced in 2015 a desire to double the percentage of young people from disadvantaged backgrounds entering university by 2020 (compared to 2009).[9]

How have the Gaps Changed over Time?

Concern over the gaps in university entry between young people from different family backgrounds would perhaps be less if the gaps had been falling over time. (We restrict attention in this section and the next one just to entry to higher education, putting to one side for the moment other aspects of university success.) It might be thought that the gaps in university entry have indeed fallen—that the big expansion in higher education since the Second World War would have favoured those from more disadvantaged families. But the opposite has been the case for much of the period. Figure 1.5 divides young people into two groups

[8] This process is described for education in general in, for example, Kaushal, N. (2013), 'Intergenerational payoffs of education', *Future of Children*, 5: 76–93.

[9] https://www.gov.uk/government/speeches/teaching-at-the-heart-of-the-system.

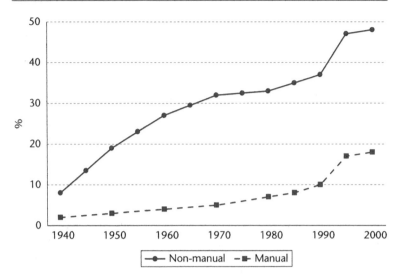

Figure 1.5. Young people entering higher education (%), by social class, 1940–2000

Note: The definition of the entry rate is the same as for the period 1961–99 in Figure 1.1.

Source: Gorard, S. (2008), 'Who is missing from higher education?' *Cambridge Journal of Education*, 38(3): 421–37, Table 8.

of social class according to parental occupation, manual and non-manual. It shows the percentage going to university by age twenty-one in each of the two groups since 1940. It is immediately apparent that the figure has risen much more for young people from non-manual family backgrounds. Over the period as a whole, the university entry rate of pupils from non-manual backgrounds increased from around 10 per cent at the end of the Second World War to nearly 50 per cent by the end of the century. By contrast, the rise for young people from manual backgrounds was to a level that was still below 20 per cent by 2000. The gap, measured as a difference between the two sets of figures, rose from about 7 percentage points to 30 percentage points.

When measured as a *ratio*, it is true that the gap fell. The non-manual entry rate—the percentage of young people from non-manual families going to university—was five to seven times higher than the manual rate over 1940–60. But by 2000 it was only about two and a half times as high. This is due to the manual rate being so low at the start of the period—when calculating the ratio in the immediate post-war period one is dividing by a very small number. The first way of measuring the gap, the *difference* between the two rates, is arguably a better guide to answering the question as to who benefited most from the expansion in higher education. Answer: young people from more advantaged family backgrounds.

A difficulty when interpreting the patterns in Figure 1.5 is that the sizes of the two social class groups change over time. The university entry rate for the 'manual' class in 2000 refers to a smaller group of young people than in 1940. The structure of occupations has changed, with many more non-manual jobs and many fewer manual jobs. In this sense, we are not really comparing like with like when looking across the sixty years covered by the graph.

Figure 1.6 overcomes this problem by showing differences in the last twenty of these years for groups that are of fixed size—the top and bottom fifths of the income distribution and the middle three-fifths. The data differ in being drawn from sample surveys rather than administrative records. They also relate to degree completion by age 23 rather than just university entry. This means that they incorporate the differences by family background in failure to complete degrees, as well as in university entry—a subject that we address later in the book in Chapter 7. But it is the differences in the entry rates that drive the pattern shown. Whether expressed as a difference between the figures or as a ratio, the gap between the percentages of young people with a degree by age 23 from the top and bottom of the income distribution

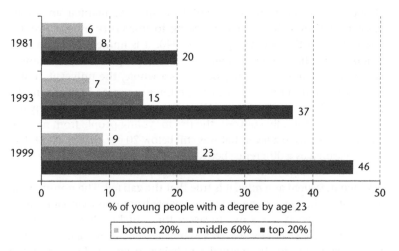

Figure 1.6. Young people with a degree by age 23 (%), by level of family income

Source: Blanden, J. and Machin, S. (2004), 'Educational inequality and the expansion of higher education', *Scottish Journal of Political Economy*, 51(2): 230–49, Table 1. Figures based on NCDS and BCS70 birth cohorts and the British Household Panel Survey.

increased substantially in the last two decades of the twentieth century. For example, the difference in the percentages jumps from 14 points in 1981 to 37 points in 1999 and the ratio from 3.3 to 5.4. And this gap was driven almost entirely by the large increase in participation rates at the top of the distribution. The percentage of young people in the bottom fifth of the income distribution with a degree by age 23 rises only from 6 per cent to 9 per cent while the figure for the top fifth increases from 20 per cent to 46 per cent.

The graph tells a much more negative story than shown for the same years in Figure 1.5. There was no rise in the gap in entry rates between manual and non-manual families between 1980 and 2000 in Figure 1.5. And, notably, there was a marked rise in the rate for young people from manual families—in contrast to the story told by Figure 1.6 for young people from the bottom fifth of the income distribution, who did not see an increase in their participation rate (although the rate did increase for those from the middle three-fifths). Part of the explanation for the differences between the two figures may lie in the different definition of family background—income and occupation are not the same thing. Moreover, the twenty years covered in Figure 1.6 were a period when the distribution of income widened markedly. The bottom fifth and top fifths moved much further apart. So in this sense, like is again not being compared with like if we contrast the start of the 1980s with the end of the 1990s. Or the explanation may lie in one of the other differences between the two sets of data.[10]

We cannot easily resolve the differences in these two accounts of the years from 1980 to 2000. But taken together, the two graphs agree on one important message: there is no evidence that family background gaps in university entry, at least when measured as differences between groups, became substantially less towards the end of the twentieth century.

What about differences in rates of entry to 'high status' universities? The period since the Second World War saw at least two major changes in the structure of UK higher education relevant to the status of different institutions in the system. The first followed the Robbins Report of 1963, which we have already referred to as a landmark. A major expansion of higher education followed the recommendations of Lord Robbins' committee. But this did not happen through existing or new universities, as Robbins had recommended. Rather, it took place

---

[10] For a discussion of the different pictures that emerge from comparing mobility across generations using occupation or income, see Blanden, J., Gregg, P., and Macmillan, L. (2013), 'Intergenerational persistence in income and social class: the effect of within-group inequality', *Journal of the Royal Statistical Society*, Series A, 176: 541–63.

through the creation of polytechnics, administered by local authorities and awarding degrees accredited by a new central authority. Polytechnics were originally intended to focus on vocational degree courses, although they increasingly offered academic courses as well over time. Their creation led to the so-called 'binary divide' between these new institutions and the older universities.

This binary divide was formally removed in 1992 when the polytechnics were all transformed into universities, free from local control and awarding their own degrees. But many of the 'new' or 'post-1992' universities not surprisingly remain different in various respects to many of the 'old' or 'pre-1992' universities. None of the 'high status' universities identified in Table 1.1 are former polytechnics. These distinctions between different institutions—in terms of the experiences they offer and the returns that their graduates receive—continue to be relevant even now, some twenty-five years after the abolition of the binary divide, and it is these differences that justify our focus on the type of institution attended by students from different socio-economic backgrounds, as well as whether they go to university at all.[11]

How do the Gaps Compare with those in Other Countries?

Our concern might also be less if the gaps in entry to university between young people from different backgrounds were notably lower in the UK than those in other countries. At least by this yardstick, the UK would be doing well. Not perfectly by any means, but it could then be argued that we are doing better than elsewhere.

Other countries certainly have substantial family background gaps too—both in rates of entry to any higher education and in entry to higher status institutions among those who do go to university. The UK is very far from being unique in this respect. The situation in the USA, for example, has been well documented and much of the relevant information is readily available. But a brief inspection of some of the data shows that comparison with the UK is not straightforward.

Figure 1.7 shows the percentage of US high school graduates in 2010 who immediately went on to enrol in two-year or four-year colleges, distinguishing between the bottom fifth of the income distribution, the top fifth, and the middle three-fifths. Whereas over 80 per cent of young

---

[11] For discussion of how current views of what are high status and other universities relates to the old binary divide, see Boliver, V. (2015), 'Are there distinctive clusters of higher and lower status universities in the UK?' *Oxford Review of Education*, 41(5): 608–27.

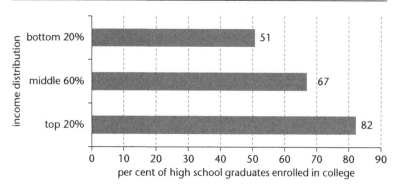

Figure 1.7. Entry rates to college (%), by high school graduates in the USA by level of family income, 2010

Note: The figures refer to the percentage of high school completers aged 16–24 who were enrolled in 2- or 4-year colleges the October immediately following high school completion.

Source: Aud, S., Hussar, W., Johnson, F., Kena, G., Roth, E., Manning, E., Wang, X., and Zhang, J. (2012), *The Condition of Education 2012* (NCES 2012–045), U.S. Department of Education, National Center for Education Statistics. Washington, DC, Indicator 34 Table A-34-1.

people from the top income group go straight on to college, the figure for the bottom fifth is much lower, only about 50 per cent.

The gaps implied by the graph are large, but they might appear at first sight to be somewhat lower than in the UK—Figure 1.6 showed a difference of 37 percentage points between graduation rates for young people from the bottom and top fifths of the income distribution. And the success of the US system in getting as many as half of those from the bottom fifth into college is also striking. This is far more than in the UK, it would seem.

However, this contrast illustrates the difficulty with international comparisons and the problems of securing comparable data. First, the US figures are restricted to high school graduates only. But one in four young people in the USA do not complete high school. Unsurprisingly, the figure is much higher for those from disadvantaged family backgrounds and lower for those from advantaged backgrounds. Taking this into account, survey data for around 1990 suggest that only about 20 per cent of teenagers from families in the bottom quarter of the income distribution entered college, compared to 70 per cent of those from the top quarter—an enormous difference.[12]

---

[12] These figures come from Table 2.6 of Haveman, R. and Wilson, K. (2007), 'Access, Matriculation, and Graduation', in Dickert-Conlin, S. and Rubenstein, R. (eds), *Economic*

Second, the UK data in Figure 1.6 refer to the percentage getting a degree by age 23. When the US survey data just cited are also restricted to the percentage who graduate, the figures fall to about 6 per cent for the bottom quarter of the income distribution and 40 per cent for the top quarter, similar to the figures for the UK in 1999 for the bottom and top fifths of the income distribution. As this underlines, drop-out is a major feature of higher education in the USA, right across the income distribution, and—as we shall show in Chapter 7—a much larger problem than in the UK.

Third, the US figures in the graph refer to entry to either two-year colleges, known as 'community colleges', or four-year colleges. The former lead to an 'associate degree'. The latter lead to a Bachelor's degree, although the situation is complicated by the community colleges also acting partly as feeders for the four-year colleges, with some of their graduates entering the latter in the second or third year of the four-year course. Courses at four-year colleges are much more comparable with the three- or four-year undergraduate degree courses in the UK, and they lead to better jobs—the four-year colleges are of much higher status. College status is certainly a very prominent issue in the USA. Teenagers from higher income families are much more likely to go to four-year colleges. In 2005, nearly a third of 18–24 year olds from families in the bottom fifth of the income distribution who were enrolled in college were in two-year colleges, compared to less than a fifth of those enrolled from families in the richest fifth.[13] And among the four-year colleges there are huge differences in status, again associated in part with the financial return on education that they provide. For example, the 'Ivy League'—eight rich private universities in the northeast of the USA—is a well-known elite set of institutions. More broadly, US colleges are often classified according to the extent to which their student entry is selective and family background gaps are much larger the more selective is the university's entry requirements.[14]

Inequality and Higher Education, New York: Russell Sage Foundation. They are based on the Panel Survey of Income Dynamics with income adjusted for family needs. The data in Figure 1.5 are based on the Current Population Survey and are not adjusted in this way.

[13] These figures are drawn from the Current Population Survey 2005, Table 14 (http://www.census.gov/hhes/school/data/cps/2005/tab14-06.xls). We have used the figures for families with less than $30,000 and with $100,000 or more which roughly correspond to the bottom and top fifths of the distribution.

[14] For example, see the study by Carnevale and Rose summarized in Table 2 of Haveman, R. and Smeeding, T. (2006), 'The role of higher education in social mobility', *The Future of Children*, 16(2): 125–49.

16

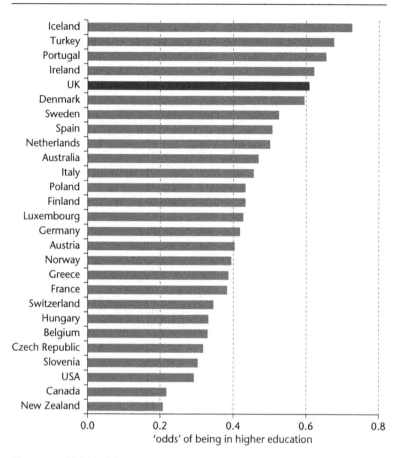

Figure 1.8. 'Odds' of being in higher education for young people aged 20–34 with parents with low levels of education, 2009

Note: See text for definition of 'odds'.

Source: OECD (2012), *Education at a Glance*, Paris: OECD, Table A6.1.

This analysis of figures for the UK and the USA serves as a warning that comparisons across countries of the things we would like to compare are not easily undertaken. Nevertheless, attempts have been made by international organizations to put data from a range of countries on a common basis. Figure 1.8 shows the results of an analysis of data from 2009 by the Organisation for Economic Co-operation and Development (OECD), which includes most of the world's rich industrialized market economies. For twenty-seven countries, the graph compares the chances of young people being at university if their parents have low

17

levels of education, defined as not completing upper secondary education. One difficulty in making the comparisons is the large differences across countries in the percentage of parents in the population with low education. (Essentially, this is the same problem already seen in assessing the pattern in Figure 1.5 where there was a change over the period in the relative importance of manual and non-manual occupations in the population.) To take this into account, the OECD calculate the 'odds' of the young person being in higher education if their parents have low education. This is defined as the percentage of all 20–34 year olds in higher education with parents with a low level of education divided by the percentage of parents of this type among all parents. For the UK the two figures are 25 per cent and 42 per cent. Dividing the first by the second yields an 'odds' of around 0.6, highlighted in the graph.

The odds would be equal to one were the share of the young people in higher education from this type of family background to be equal to the share of their parents among the population of all parents. The graph shows clearly that under-representation is, unsurprisingly, ubiquitous—the odds are everywhere less than one. Having a parent with a low level of education reduces the chances of being in higher education in each and every country. But the graph also shows that the odds for the UK are high by the standards of many other countries, and by implication that the UK is more equal in terms of university access than many other countries. The UK ranks as high as fifth, behind only Ireland, Portugal, Turkey, and Iceland in the apparent success in entering higher education of young people from more disadvantaged family backgrounds, in terms of parental education. The odds in the UK are far higher than in Canada and the USA for example, which are down at the bottom of the graph with odds of around 0.2 and 0.3, or even France and Germany with odds of below 0.4.

Despite the OECD's best efforts to base the figures on comparable data, however, difficulties in the comparisons remain. The OECD is careful to note that typically the data contain young people studying for the equivalent of the US 'associate degrees', so this is a wider definition of 'higher education' than one would wish for. But the OECD's data do not include this group in Australia, Canada, New Zealand and the USA. This will have the effect of understating the odds in these four countries in Figure 1.8—and it is notable that three of them have the lowest values in the graph. Another problem of comparison for the UK is the way parental education is defined. It is not clear for example how one should classify the parents who left school at sixteen, something much more common among their generation than it is today—around half of parents of 20–34 year olds would have done so. Should all these parents be considered as failing to complete 'upper secondary education', even if they left school with good passes in age 16 public exams? The treatment in the data is unclear.[15]

More generally, the standardization of the data with the 'odds' calculation clearly helps, but there is a limit to what can be achieved when the share of all parents with a low education varies so much across the countries—from about 10 per cent in Norway and Finland to over 80 per cent in Portugal and Turkey. There appear to be no data that would allow a simple comparison of university entry in the UK with other rich countries using groups of the same size, such as the bottom and top 20 per cent of the income distribution, as in Figure 1.6.

What can we conclude? Our view is fairly cautious given the difficulties in comparison across countries that we have underlined. First, we can certainly say, as in the film *E.T.*, that 'we are not alone'. Large family background gaps exist elsewhere. Second, the UK is probably not among the worst countries, although where exactly we come in a league table is hard to establish with any certainty. That we are not alone suggests firmly that there are common causes across countries, as well as the explanation lying in particular institutional details of the education system in the UK—whether the financing of higher education, the degree of autonomy that universities have in selecting students (high in the UK compared to many other countries), or any other feature.

What Does this Book Do?

The scene for our book has now been set. But the family background gaps in university success that we are concerned with are long-standing, are mostly well known (at least as far as university entry is concerned), and have been the subject of much research already. What is distinctive about our approach? And what do we add that is new?

First, we draw on *quantitative* evidence. This is the information contained in data from national surveys and administrative records that measure the extent of the family background gaps in university entry and other aspects of university success and the factors associated with them. This approach complements the analysis of other types of evidence, notably from qualitative data collected from focus groups and in-depth interviews with young people and their families. The

---

[15] See the discussion of this point in Atkinson, A., Cantillon, B., Marlier, E., and Nolan, B. (2002), *Social Indicators. The EU and Social Inclusion*, Oxford: Oxford University Press.

quantitative evidence we discuss is largely from our own research, much of it conducted with the financial support of the Nuffield Foundation.

Second, we focus where possible on the evidence for *England*. England is an interesting country in which to study socio-economic differences in university entry and outcomes, for at least two reasons. It has made dramatic changes to the way in which undergraduate higher education is financed over the last decade—substantially increasing tuition fees, but also changing the amount and composition of student support in the form of grants and loans, as we shall see in Chapter 3.[16] And focusing on England offers us access to outstanding data. Administrative records from schools and universities, linked together, allow us to follow pupils from the age of five, as they enter formal schooling, right through to university and indeed graduation and beyond. Such comprehensive longitudinal data enable us to gain a better understanding of the drivers of participation in higher education and the impact of introducing changes to the way in which universities' teaching is financed. For both of these reasons, our spotlight is therefore on England, although we make some comparisons with the rest of the UK at suitable points, notably in Chapter 3. We also make some limited comparisons, where appropriate, with the evidence for other rich industrialized countries, mindful of the difficulties of international comparison that we have noted.

Third, we analyse a great deal of recent data and recent policy changes. Our analysis is as *up-to-date* as we can make it. In our scene setting, we have cited figures from before the first of the two recent major changes in university fees, in 2006/7 and 2012/13. But these changes in the funding of undergraduate education are central to our analysis. Almost all our data come from the twenty-first century, not the twentieth. We use these data to shed new light on the implications of the major changes in tuition fees and student maintenance about which there has been so much concern. But in doing so we aim also to see whether family background gaps are still driven by factors that have long been identified as important—notably the differences in attainment between children from different backgrounds during primary and secondary schooling. We also look forward, where possible, highlighting areas where research provides lessons that may be useful to policymakers dealing with issues of current and future concern, such

---

[16] Education is a 'devolved' issue in the UK, meaning that there is not just one system and set of policies for the whole country. There are substantial differences between the routes taken by the devolved authorities in Scotland, Wales and Northern Ireland, both in terms of higher education funding and the education system more generally, which are relevant to our story. This also provides further motivation for our focus on England, rather than Great Britain (England, Wales and Scotland) or the UK (Great Britain plus Northern Ireland).

as the size and scope of the higher education sector and the thorny issue of how best to fund it.

Fourth, we look beyond entry to university to analyse socio-economic differences in outcomes at and indeed after university as well—the family background gaps in other aspects of 'university success' that we underlined earlier in this chapter. We know that the benefits of higher education typically relate to degree acquisition—to actually having a degree. Moreover, as we touched on earlier in the chapter, these benefits vary by the type of institution attended and indeed the degree class with which individuals leave university. This raises the question: is getting more students from poorer families into higher education enough? Or do policymakers and indeed universities need to focus efforts to reduce socio-economic inequalities beyond the point at which students apply to university for higher education to truly 'level the playing field' between those from different backgrounds? Our book is novel in bringing together the analysis of the family background gaps in university entry, in drop-out and degree completion, in degree class, and in outcomes following graduation. This provides for a much fuller picture.

We proceed as follows. Chapter 2 reviews the reasons why governments subsidize the teaching function of universities and the ways in which this can be done. We compare three methods: 'free' university for students (funded by general taxation), a system of fees and loans (as at present), and a tax on graduates. Chapter 3 then lays out as simply as we can the essential details of the higher education funding system in England, and in particular the major changes that occurred in 2006/7 and 2012/13. What exactly is this sea change that has taken place, viewed from the perspective of young people and their families having to decide about whether to try to go to university and of graduates emerging with loans to repay? We also show how the system in England compares with that in the rest of the UK and in other countries. Chapter 4 goes on to analyse how family background gaps in England in application and entry to university, and in the status of university entered, have changed over the last 10–15 years—a period that spans the two big funding reforms.

The fact that large socio-economic gaps in higher education participation existed even when universities charged no tuition fees suggests that the larger costs students face when going to university cannot be the predominant driver of the gaps that we see now: there must be other factors at work. In Chapter 5 we turn to the issue that is at the heart of the matter: attainment during secondary schooling. We show just how important is 'prior attainment'—how well teenagers are doing at school *before* they get to the point at which they might apply to university. We also show that prior attainment seems to be more important in England than in some other countries. Chapter 6 goes further, exploring just how early these socio-economic gaps in attainment emerge, and what this suggests about when best to intervene to increase young people's attainment and hence their likelihood of going to university.

We then move on from socio-economic differences in participation in higher education to consider outcomes once individuals arrive at university and indeed well beyond their time as a student. In Chapter 7 we look at the relationship between family background and success while at university: avoiding drop-out, completing a degree, and the class of degree awarded to those who graduate. And in Chapter 8 we look at socio-economic differences in success amongst graduates in the labour market once they have left university.

Chapter 9 reports our conclusions, highlighting the implications of the key points we have made in earlier chapters for the main stakeholders with an interest in higher education: the government, universities, and students and their families.

We end this introduction to the book by noting two important restrictions to our analysis. The first is that our treatment of family background is limited by the definition we set ourselves. We are concerned with differences by parental education, family income, local area living standards, and type of school attended—state or private. Our definition does not extend to ethnicity. This is not because ethnic inequalities in higher education are unimportant, but—amongst students attending state schools in England at least—young people from all ethnic minority backgrounds are now, on average, more likely to go to university than their majority White British counterparts.[17] This is in marked contrast to analysis of educational differences in the USA, where the differences by race are often to the fore and where policy on 'affirmative action' attempts to reduce them.[18]

The second restriction is our focus on entry to full-time university study by young people following secondary schooling—on the traditional main entry route to higher education. People aged 20 or under accounted for nearly 80 per cent of all acceptances of places for full-time undergraduate study at UK universities in 2013 and entrants (of all ages)

---

[17] Crawford, C. and Greaves, E. (2015), *Socio-economic, ethnic and gender differences in HE participation*, Report to the Department for Business, Innovation and Skills. Some ethnic minority groups are, however, more likely to drop out of university and less likely to achieve high degree classes—see, for example, Hefce (2010), 'Student ethnicity: profile and progression of entrants to full-time first degree study', Issues Paper 2010/13.

[18] A classic study of race and university entry in the USA is provided by Bowen, W. and Bok, D. (1998), *The Shape of the River. Long-Term Consequences of Considering Race in College and University Admissions*, Princeton, NJ: Princeton University Press.

to full-time courses made up over 70 per cent of all undergraduate entrants.[19] But this means that we do not address entry by 'mature' students or part-time study other than in passing. These are important routes into higher education, and could usefully be the subject of a future book.

---

[19] UCAS (2013), *2013 Application Cycle: End of Cycle Report*, Cheltenham: UCAS, Table 5a, and Higher Education Statistics Agency website.

2

Why and How do Governments Fund Higher Education?

Why do governments involve themselves at all in subsidizing higher education? That is, why should not the entire university system—or at least its teaching function—be financed by fees charged to students? (We are not concerned in this book with universities' research activity.) Some of the arguments were alluded to in Chapter 1 when we argued why gaps in university entry by family background 'matter'. But here we start by reviewing them systematically.

This deals with the first part of the question in the title to the chapter, *why* fund teaching in universities. We then move on to discuss the second part, *how* governments can support universities' teaching costs. In particular, we explain why a system of charging fees to students and then offering them loans to cover those fees—the current policy in England—can be part of a sensible solution, given that a key aim of governments is to reduce the gaps by family background in going to university. We compare three policies: (i) no fees, where university is 'free' and funded out of general taxation; (ii) charging fees and offering a loan—where the precise form of the loan turns out to be crucial; and (iii) a policy of no fees again, but with the costs of teaching covered by imposing a tax on students after they have finished university—a so-called 'graduate tax'.[1]

---

[1] The case for government intervention and the form that it can take are discussed in more detail in Chapter 12 of Barr, N. (2012), *The Economics of the Welfare State* (5th edn), Oxford: Oxford University Press, and Barr, N. (2010), 'Paying for higher education: What policies, in what order?' Submission to the Independent Review of Higher Education Funding and Student Finance (the Browne Review).

Why Subsidize Teaching in Universities?

It is widely acknowledged that the 'private returns' to higher education—the gains for the individual who goes to university—are high on average, in both the UK and other countries. The evidence for this, in terms of the additional earnings accrued by graduates, was described in Chapter 1. Individuals also gain in other ways besides the salary of a graduate job, again mentioned in Chapter 1.

But there is also strong evidence that higher education confers a range of benefits to society as a whole, over and above the gains that accrue to individuals. The 'social returns' to higher education include the economic growth that a better skilled workforce brings, more tax revenue, less expenditure on benefits for the unemployed and for low-paid workers, a supply of trained doctors and teachers, and the transmission of culture across generations.[2] These outcomes represent the 'positive externalities'—the benefits for others—that result from individuals' decisions to go to university. They justify governments providing some subsidy to universities' teaching costs—the universities are training individuals who will benefit society.

A second reason for government intervention is what economists call failures in credit markets—the market for loans. Imagine that governments did not fund university teaching and that students had to pay fees to cover all the costs. With credit markets that function perfectly, students could borrow money to cover the fees and then pay back the loan from future income. But the promise of a degree is generally not sufficient collateral on which to get a loan from banks. There is no physical collateral that can be offered against the loan—unlike when borrowing to finance the purchase of a house. It is very hard for lenders to predict which students are likely to do well out of investing in a degree, and hence pay back their loan, and which students are not. This problem of what is known as 'adverse selection' means that lenders will have to charge high interest rates or impose other conditions on loans, such as rationing their availability or requiring guarantors for the loan in order to supply them. The overall effect is that there would be too few loans made—a form of economic 'inefficiency'. That is, there would be too little higher education for society's benefit.

---

[2] The social benefits are summarized in Department of Business, Innovation and Skills (2013), *Things We Know and Don't Know about the Wider Benefits of Higher Education: A Review of the Recent Literature*. See also, for example, Willetts, D. (2015), *Funding Higher Education: Keeping the Right Balance*, London: The Policy Institute, King's College London.

In such a world of no government involvement in funding the costs of university teaching, the problems faced in securing a loan to cover tuition fees will be a particular barrier for young people from poorer families. This leads to a third reason for government intervention—a concern over equity. The parents of young people from poorer families will be much less able to stand as guarantors for loans. It may be that these students will also be more concerned about the risk and uncertainty over the financial return to their studies. What would happen if they failed their degree? What happens if the return to their degree is less than anticipated? This situation will help create differences by family background in entry to university. We argued in Chapter 1 that these family background gaps matter. Without at least some government intervention (intervention that might be targeted only on poorer families), the link between family origins and destination in adult life will be stronger and social mobility lower than would otherwise be the case.

To this point we have considered only the costs of providing teaching. Unless universities are available everywhere across the country, at least some students will have to live away from home in order to benefit from higher education. Funding teaching in higher education means not just funding the supply of teaching but also funding students to live independently away from home so as to be able to access that teaching. All three reasons for governments funding at least some of universities' teaching costs may also lead governments to provide support to help cover students' living costs. In the absence of such support, many students, especially those from poorer backgrounds, may be restricted in their choice of university. This will matter if, as can be expected, universities are not all of a similar quality and do not all offer the same range of courses. Even if universities were all identical and available everywhere across the country, an argument for government support for student living costs could still be made on the grounds that parents, especially poorer ones, should not have to support their adult children.

There is no doubt that there is a clear role for governments in funding higher education and in supporting students through university. The issue for the rest of this chapter is what form that role should take. We now turn to discuss the *how* in the chapter's title.

'Free' University

When going to university was still relatively unusual, governments could afford to pay for all direct costs of higher education. Broadly speaking, that is what governments did in England and the rest of the UK during much of the post-war period. And they did so for anyone going to university, at least as far as tuition was concerned. There were no tuition fees, and 'maintenance' grants—money to cover living expenses—to support a student away from home were made available to any young person getting a university place, means-tested on family income. These grants did not have to be repaid on graduation. Universities' teaching costs and maintenance grants were funded out of general taxation.[3]

This system did not mean that governments wrote a blank cheque for universities' teaching costs. Until very recently—we give details in Chapter 3—governments have controlled the supply of university places. The ways in which this has been done have changed over the years, as has the degree to which control has been exercised—one of the key influences on the trend in student enrolment shown in Figure 1.1. 'Free' university in England meant free to those who were allowed in, not free to all comers.

Some people believe fervently that the policy of university being 'free' was and still is the appropriate one. Appropriate in the sense that education is viewed as a human right and that if a person has demonstrated that they are capable of going to university then they and their family should not have to pay for it.

Other people do not agree with this position. They accept that education should be free of charge for minors, but question whether this should be the case for young adults in higher education. Results from the British Social Attitudes survey show that there is now in fact broad acceptance of the principle of charging for university tuition among the general public—almost 80 per cent of adults in England in 2013 agreed that at least some students or their families should pay fees.[4] The large family background gaps in going to university that have always existed mean that the funding of all university education from general taxation is regressive, favouring higher income families. Viewed in this way, 'free' university is seen as part of the middle classes' so-called capture of the welfare state.

---

[3] We tell a simplified story in the interests of conveying the essentials of the system prior to the late 1990s. Post-war university fees were relatively modest and many local authorities provided assistance with paying them. The 1962 Education Act then mandated the local authorities to do so on a means-tested basis. From 1977, no student in receipt of a mandatory award paid fees, irrespective of parental income. For details see Wilson, W. (1997), 'Student grants, loans and tuition fees', House of Commons Library Research Paper 97/119. In 1962/3, student fees provided 10 per cent of higher education funding (The Robbins Report (1963), *Higher Education. Report of the Committee appointed by the Prime Minister under the Chairmanship of Lord Robbins*. London: HMSO, Table 58).

[4] Ormston, R. and Paterson, L. (2015), 'Higher Education', in Ormston, R. and Curtice, J. (eds), *British Social Attitudes: the 32nd Report*, London: NatCen Social Research.

One defence of 'free' university that is frequently offered in response to this alternative view is that a progressive income tax system means that graduates, on average, will pay more in tax anyway. As we have shown in Chapter 1, on average graduates earn substantially more than those not going to university. A second defence made is that there are important benefits to society from university education that go beyond those to the individual, as we have noted above. The argument is that these social benefits compensate for the regressive nature of the funding of 'free' university education. However, much of the benefit from university is undoubtedly 'private', accruing to the individual in the form of increased earnings and the other advantages of being a graduate that were touched on in Chapter 1. The case then follows that the individual should bear at least some of the cost of acquiring higher education.

Governments everywhere have had to weigh up the arguments on both sides of the debate in the face of increasing numbers of people going to university, in part as a result of deliberate policies of expansion. In some countries, higher education continues to be provided free of charge. In Chapter 3, we describe how the situation varies across a range of rich industrialized countries in Europe and elsewhere.

In the UK, after university enrolment expanded sharply in the 1980s and 1990s, government support for the old funding model began to break down. Public funding per student in higher education halved in the 20 years from 1980 while student numbers doubled.[5] Governments no longer had the will to continue funding undergraduate university education almost entirely from general taxation. The search was on for a method of shifting some of the cost to students. This would reflect the move to a mass higher education system. The Labour government elected in 1997 famously adopted a target of 50 per cent of young people going to university. This particular target may or may not have been sensible but it certainly was in line with the modern reality that a large fraction of each cohort now enters higher education—both as a result of rising demand and an increased supply of places. The new method of funding teaching costs would also reflect the private benefit of higher education. But at the same time it had to try to ensure that there were no financial barriers to going to university for qualified students from poorer backgrounds. The system that was adopted, after a number of policy twists and turns along the way, is to charge tuition fees and at the same time to offer student loans to cover both fees and living expenses.

---

[5] See Figure 1 in Greenaway, D. and Haynes, M. (2003), 'Funding higher education in the UK: the role of fees and loans', *The Economic Journal*, 113 (February), F150–66; and The Dearing Report (1997), *Higher Education in the Learning Society*, London: HMSO, Chart 3.16.

How can Fees and Loans be Part of a Sensible Policy?

If poorer families find it hard to obtain a loan to finance a child through university, as we argued earlier when discussing why governments intervene at all in the funding of higher education, how can a system of fees with loans be part of any sensible policy of student funding? The answer lies in the form of the loan.

The terms of a typical commercial loan are unforgiving. The borrower takes on an obligation to pay back a certain amount each month, irrespective of his or her capacity to pay. The debt is never written off, except though bankruptcy. Similar features apply to debt run up on a credit card. A minimum amount must be paid off each month and the interest rate is often high. These sorts of loans, known usually as 'mortgage-style' loans, have little part to play in any well-designed system of undergraduate student finance.

The loans for university tuition and living expenses that have been developed in the UK since the late 1990s are known as 'income-contingent' loans. Income-contingent loans are provided by a government or its agency and they start to be repaid only on graduation and only when the individual has sufficient income. The loans typically have five features:

- re-payments start when annual income exceeds a given level and are set as a percentage of income rather than a fixed monthly amount;
- no re-payments are made if the individual has income beneath the annual threshold for re-payment;
- re-payments are collected through payroll deduction alongside the income tax system;
- borrowers are charged a rate of interest that may be subsidized or may be equal only to the government's cost of borrowing;
- the debt is written off after a given number of years.

Income-contingent loans are a method of student finance with roots that extend at least as far back as the 1950s with analysis in the USA by Milton Friedman. Another early proposal was put by Alan Prest to Lord Robbins for his 1963 report on higher education in the UK.[6] This form of loan for university fees was first introduced on a national scale in

---

[6] See Chapman, B., Higgins, T., and Stiglitz, J. (eds) (2014), *Income Contingent Loans. Theory, Practice and Policy*, Basingstoke: Palgrave Macmillan; Willetts, D. (2013), *Robbins Revisited*, London: The Social Market Foundation.

Australia in 1989 and is now used in a number of other countries besides the UK.

The basic idea is that students pay no fees at the point of entry to university, that their repayment of the loan only starts—and only continues—when they have sufficient income to make a re-payment, and that the debt cannot forever hang over someone's head. It is sometimes emphasized that it is *graduates* who therefore pay for their higher education and not *students*, and this rightly highlights the key notion that the system ensures that students do not have to produce tuition fees up-front. But of course graduates are all former students and the prospect of the future debt repayment is something they will have had to consider when choosing whether or not to go to university.

In the current system of income-contingent loans in England, which we describe in more detail in Chapter 3, students are permitted to borrow an amount equal to the tuition fee that they face each year, plus an amount to contribute towards their annual living costs. All students, regardless of family income, can borrow the full amount of their tuition fee. However, the size of the loan that may be taken to cover living costs depends on family income.

This thumb-nail sketch hides details that are fleshed out in Chapter 3. The devil in part lies in those details. Nevertheless, the key features just outlined are enough to show that student debt of the form implied by income-contingent loans is quite different to debt from a bank loan or a credit card. Chapter 3 also describes the extent in practice to which the loans made to students are expected to be written off in the future, an important part of the subsidy to university teaching that the system of funding higher education in England continues to include.

A Graduate Tax

A system of fees and of loans to cover them is not the only way in which graduates can be made to contribute to the cost of their higher education but not have to face paying fees on entry to university. Another possibility is to charge no fees and to cover the cost of providing teaching in universities through a tax levied on graduates. Graduates would thus pay higher deductions from their earnings than non-graduates receiving the same salary, once their earnings cross a certain threshold. (As an alternative, the tax could be levied on all incomes rather than just earnings from employment or self-employment.) The cost of providing grants to help fund students' living expenses could also be financed in this way.

Debate over a graduate tax ranges across many different questions.[7] Would all the tax revenue really be directed towards university teaching, as should be the case with a so-called 'hypothecated' tax? What to do about students from European Union (EU) countries who return home after their studies? On the face of it, under EU law they would be charged no fee, like UK students, but would then pay no graduate tax having left the country. Would the tax provide an incentive to UK students to work abroad? What to do about students who drop out before they graduate—would there even be an incentive to drop out? Where would the incentive be for universities to improve the quality of their teaching, given that their additional costs could not be reimbursed through charging higher fees?

The issue of concern to this book is how potential university students would view a graduate tax and hence what would be its impact on family background gaps in university entry and success. From their perspective, one key difference compared to a system of fees and income-contingent loans would be that—in its simplest form—a graduate tax would be paid 'forever'. If the tax were levied on earnings from employment or self-employment, rather than on all income, it would be similar to the liability to National Insurance contributions, lasting until retirement from the workforce. A highly-paid graduate might pay far more graduate tax than he or she would when repaying an income-contingent loan—repayments that would only go on for a limited period until the debt were repaid. (By the same token, deductions from individuals' earnings with a system of income-contingent loans are linked to the exact charges for tuition that they incur at the universities which they attend—studying at universities that charge higher fees leads to a larger debt and higher deductions.) However, it would not be impossible to devise a system in which a graduate tax was limited in duration.

But perhaps the biggest difference lies in the name—a tax rather than a loan to be re-paid. As Nick Barr has put it:

> The term graduate tax moves the idea of a graduate contribution from the credit card bit of people's brains to the payroll deduction bit . . . A parent whose child has £20,000 of credit card debt rightly has sleepless nights . . . [But] parents do not worry about their child's future tax bill.[8]

---

[7] The range is illustrated in the title of a paper from the Institute of Directors, '20 reasons why a graduate tax is a bad idea'.

[8] Barr, N. (2010), 'A properly designed "graduate contribution" could work well for UK students and higher education—even though the original "graduate tax" proposal is a terrible idea': http://blogs.lse.ac.uk, 20 August.

Although the debt incurred by taking on an income-contingent loan is clearly not like credit card debt, inevitably many students and their families may still associate this form of 'debt' with all the negative connotations that the word can convey. Of course, 'tax' may also have a negative overtone, but not one of an outstanding stock of money to be repaid. It is possible that for individuals who are particularly averse to taking on debt, a graduate tax would create less of a disincentive to go to university than a system of fees and income-contingent loans.

Summing Up

There are good reasons why governments provide at least some funding for the teaching functions of universities. Such funding provides a broad range of benefits to society, increases economic efficiency, and furthers equity.

The ways in which that funding can be provided (and its extent) are matters for debate. This chapter has reviewed the arguments for providing 'free' university, for charging fees repaid by a particular form of loan, and for a graduate tax. Chapter 3 investigates in more detail the method that has now been adopted in England—fees and income-contingent loans.

3

How is University Teaching Funded in England?

Sensational headlines have been used to describe changes to higher education funding policy in England in recent years. The stories beneath them have focused on the sharp increase in maximum tuition fees that universities can charge for their undergraduate teaching, rising from less than £3,500 to £9,000 per year in 2012, and the associated increase in student debt. Typical titles include 'Today's graduates face years with debt around their necks' and 'Students could be paying back loans into their 50s'. In this chapter we explain the funding of universities' undergraduate teaching in England and the support given to students with both their tuition fees and living costs. What, in practice, is the system of fees and 'income contingent' loans—for both tuition fees and maintenance—that has been adopted in England? And how does the system in England compare to that in other rich industrialized countries?

The chapter then shows in more detail how financial support for *students* varies for young people with different levels of parental income. How much support do students from lower-income families receive? We then turn to look at the consequences for *graduates* of the changes in the system behind the newspaper headlines. How much, across their working lives, will graduates be paying back in loan repayments? And how does this vary—how much will graduates with high lifetime earnings repay and what about graduates who earn much less? This provides the backdrop to Chapter 4, which explores whether the financial support available to students from different backgrounds affects their decision to go to university, and in particular whether it has increased the gap in participation between young people from lower and higher socio-economic backgrounds that we saw in Chapter 1.

Funding for Teaching and Student Support in England

For students, the overall cost of going to university in England comprises the direct costs of studying (such as any tuition fees charged, and books and course materials that they must purchase) and living costs if they live away from the family home. The great majority of young people following undergraduate courses in England do leave home in order to study. In the mid-1980s, less than one in ten young, full-time students lived with their parents in their first year at university and the figure was still only about one in five by 2006/7.[1] For most students, going to university therefore brings substantial housing and other costs of independent living as well as fees. (Of course, young people would face analogous living costs if they did not go to university and worked away from home but their wages would be expected to cover these expenses.)

As we noted in Chapter 2, supporting students' living costs allows them to choose from universities across the country and this can be viewed as an important and long-standing feature of 'university culture' in the UK. The funding of higher education in England therefore focuses not only on how universities are funded to deliver teaching, but also on how students are supported financially while they are studying.[2] Both aspects have undergone a dramatic transformation over the last twenty-five years.[3] Prior to 1998, there were no fees and universities relied on government grants to cover their costs of teaching. Students were eligible for 'means-tested' maintenance grants—grants assessed on the level of their family's income—to cover part of their living costs. From 1990, they could also take out 'mortgage-style' loans of the type described in Chapter 2 to provide further help with living costs (the loans again depending on family income).

By the turn of the twenty-first century, however, many more young people were entering university and successive UK governments decided that it was no longer practical or equitable to fund the teaching function of universities wholly from general taxation. Tuition fees were therefore introduced. They were first charged to students in England in 1998, at

---

[1] Hefce (2009), 'Patterns in Higher Education: Living at Home', Issues paper, June 2009/20.

[2] Universities also receive grants from the government to fund research and other activities, including work to increase the participation, retention, and advancement of groups who are currently under-represented in higher education, such as those from disadvantaged backgrounds. These are outside the scope of this book, however.

[3] The various twists and turns up until 2009 can be followed in Wyness, G. (2010), 'Policy changes in UK higher education funding, 1963–2009', Department of Quantitative Social Science Working Paper 10-05, UCL Institute of Education.

£1,000 a year, which had to be paid up-front, although those from poor families (with incomes below £22,500 per year) were exempt. Since 2006, all students have been liable for higher tuition fees, but these fees are deferred: no payment has to be made on starting university or in subsequent years of study, provided students take a loan offered by the government to cover the fees. As we will see later, many governments elsewhere have chosen not to charge fees for higher education, or have set fees at a much lower level, by implication retaining what is probably a substantially higher rate of public subsidy for university teaching.

But for the moment we need to explain in a little more detail how the system of higher education funding and support for students works in England. In a nutshell, the funding system since 2006 has involved various transfers of money flowing between the government, universities, students, and graduates—see Figure 3.1.

Universities receive grants from the government to cover part of the cost of teaching undergraduates. They also receive tuition fees from students. The number of students that each university could admit was controlled until 2015/16, thus placing a limit on the extent of government funding. The controls were relaxed progressively, beginning in 2012/13 when universities were allowed to take as many students as they wished with excellent A-level results.[4]

Students receive various forms of support. They get loans from the government to cover all of their tuition fees ('fee loans') and part of their living costs ('maintenance loans'). Maintenance loans depend on the

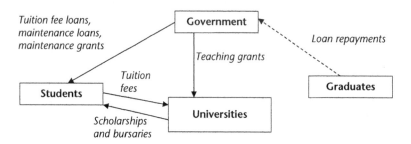

Figure 3.1. Funding for undergraduate teaching and student support in England

Note: Universities also receive grants from the government to fund research and other activities, including work to increase the participation, retention, and advancement of groups who are currently under-represented in higher education, including those from disadvantaged backgrounds.

[4] In 2012/13, the A-level threshold was at least two A grades and a B grade, reduced to at least one A and two B grades the following year.

level of family income, with the smallest loans going to students from the richest families. Until 2016, students from lower income families also received means-tested maintenance grants from the government, which did not have to be repaid. (In 2016, maintenance grants were replaced by slightly higher maintenance loans for the poorest students. The grants have been retained for students who started their studies in earlier years.) Students from lower income families may also receive cash bursaries (again non-repayable) or fee-waivers from their university—this is represented by the line in Figure 3.1 going from 'universities' to 'students'. The support varies from university to university and may also cover students who are not from low-income families, such as those with high A-level scores or from areas with low rates of university entry.

Graduates repay their loan debt to the government when their income rises above a given threshold. Repayments must also be made by students who drop-out of university before completing their degrees, a group we consider in Chapter 7. The eventual repayment may only be partial as debts are written off in certain circumstances, including after a fixed period—for this reason we have drawn a dotted line in Figure 3.1 from 'graduates' to 'government' in contrast to the solid line for loans from 'government' to 'students'.

The 2006 reforms and the subsequent changes, most notably in 2012, as well as 2016, involved varying the parameters in this system. The one that has attracted the most attention is the increase in the maximum annual tuition fee that a university can charge. In 2006 this was set to £3,000 and the figure could rise with inflation each year. As part of the 2012 reforms, the maximum fee was raised from around £3,375 per year to £9,000 per year and most universities charged this figure or close to it, but, at least until 2016, this could not rise with inflation. (At the time of writing, in early 2016, the government is consulting on allowing universities offering high-quality teaching to increase fees in line with inflation from 2017.) We discuss the implications of these changes for students from different backgrounds and graduates with different lifetime incomes in more detail below.

Students from England may be charged this maximum £9,000 fee wherever they go to university in the UK. (As we shall see below, students from other parts of the UK face somewhat different fee and student support regimes depending on where they study.) In order to charge above £6,000 per year, English universities are required to provide some support to some students (shown by the arrow in Figure 3.1 that we noted above). Each university must come up with a package of support that is approved by the Office for Fair Access (OFFA), described on its website as 'the independent public body that promote[s] and safeguard[s] fair access to higher education for people from lower income and other under-represented backgrounds'.[5]

While the 2012 reforms increased the level of tuition fees, they significantly reduced the teaching grants provided by the government to universities—the vertical line joining these two boxes in Figure 3.1. Before September 2012, teaching grants were paid by the government to universities in respect of all eligible students. The amount paid depended on the subject, ranging from £2,325 per student per year for classroom-based subjects to £13,335 for clinical years of study in medicine, dentistry, and veterinary science. Since then, however, only students in these clinical years of study and 'laboratory-based science, engineering and technology' (around one in four full-time undergraduates) have attracted substantive teaching grants, at lower rates of around £10,000 and £1,500 per year respectively in 2015.[6]

Universities, on average, benefited as a result of these reforms. We estimate that funding per young full-time undergraduate student increased by 28 per cent, on average, between 2011/12 and 2012/13.[7] But a larger share of this funding will now come from those who go to university rather than from general government spending. The apparent implication might seem to be that the government no longer believes that the 'social benefits' of the degree programmes being followed by the majority of students are worth subsidizing. But this ignores the fact that, at least on current estimates, not all graduates are expected to repay the full value of their loans.

The loan repayment terms and how they have changed over time are discussed in more detail below, but in essence graduates repay a percentage of their income above a threshold until their debt is repaid or until the end of the repayment period. As we described in Chapter 2, such income-contingent loans 'insure' graduates against part of the risk of unemployment or low pay, as they do not have to make loan repayments in these circumstances. While graduates are, on average, more likely to be in work and more likely to earn more, conditional on being in work, than individuals who have not gone to university, a large number of graduates are still expected to spend at least part of their

---

[5] http://www.offa.org.uk/.

[6] The numbers of full-time undergraduates who attract teaching grants are given in Hefce (2012), 'Student numbers from HESES and HEIFES (March 2012)', Higher Education Funding Council for England. The amount of teaching grants paid for different subjects is described in Hefce (2015), 'Guide to funding 2015–16: how Hefce allocates its funds', March 2015/04, Higher Education Funding Council for England. Intermediate cost subjects such as archaeology and computer science were also allocated teaching grants of £150 per year in 2015.

[7] Crawford, C., Crawford, R., and Jin, W. (2014), *Estimating the public cost of student loans*, IFS Report No. 94, London: Institute for Fiscal Studies.

working lives out of work or in low-paying jobs, meaning that they will make no or only low repayments in some years. Because student debts are large, periods of no or low repayments mean that a substantial proportion of graduates are not expected to repay the value of their loans in full and hence have some of their debt written off at the end of the repayment period.

These write-offs represent a substantial subsidy for higher education. The so-called 'RAB charge'—the resource accounting and budgeting charge—is the official label given to the estimate of how much of the value of each £1 the government lends out is not expected to be repaid. It is affected by three things: the loan repayment terms; estimates of graduates' incomes across their working lives; and how much the government values today the loan repayments it expects to receive in future. The size of this subsidy may come as a surprise. In March 2014 the government estimated it to be as high as 45 per cent, although, as we shall see later, it has come down somewhat since then.

Nonetheless, this subsidy means that, even after the increase in tuition fees to £9,000 per year in 2012, we estimate that the government is still expected to spend around £15,000 per student in today's money (compared to around £23,000 per student in today's money under the 2011 system). These estimates of the government's contribution to the cost of higher education are, however, highly uncertain, depending as they do on how much of the loans made by the government to students goes on to be repaid, something that will not be known for decades to come. In essence, the government has swapped a larger certain upfront cost (in the form of teaching grants) for a potentially smaller but uncertain future cost (in the form of debt write-offs), which will only be realized for each cohort once they reach the end of the repayment period. This is a radical shift in higher education funding policy.

How Does the System in England Compare with that Elsewhere?

What choices about fees and public subsidies to university teaching have governments made in other countries? Are the arrangements in England so very different from those elsewhere?

The obvious place to start answering these questions is close to home—in the other parts of the UK. The devolved administrations in Scotland, Wales and Northern Ireland make their own decisions on university fees. We focus on Scotland and Wales and describe the situation prevailing in late 2015.

Scotland charges no fees at all at Scottish universities to students from families resident in Scotland. European Union (EU) law requires the same zero fee for students coming from other EU countries.[8] But students from the rest of the UK are charged fees up to the same £9,000 maximum that they would face in England. Scottish students coming south of the border face the same fees as English students (and the Scottish government does not contribute to paying these fees). But around 95 per cent of Scottish young people going to university stay in Scotland and already did so before 2012. The 2012 reforms therefore left the cost of going to university unchanged for the great majority of Scottish students—a cost in terms of tuition fees of zero.

Students from families living in Wales do contribute to the cost of their tuition at Welsh universities, but at the old level that prevailed in England before 2012 of about £3,500 per year, adjusted upwards only for inflation. And if they go to university elsewhere in the UK and hence face a fee of up to £9,000 per year, the Welsh administration pays the difference. In other words, the 2012 changes brought virtually no change in fees for Welsh students. Students from England or elsewhere in the UK face the £9,000 maximum at Welsh universities.

The Welsh and, in particular, the Scottish administrations have therefore made different choices. How do they afford this? The funding picture is complicated by the implicit subsidy to Welsh and Scottish students studying within their own nations by the higher fees paid by English students at university in Wales and Scotland. In 2013/14, around 20 per cent of first year full-time undergraduates in Scotland were from England while the figure was 30 per cent in Wales.[9] Scottish and Welsh universities can charge these students up to £9,000 per year. But the universities' main funding comes via expenditure from block grants from Westminster based on the 'Barnett formula' that figured in debate before the referendum on Scottish independence in 2014. From these grants, the Scottish and Welsh governments fund higher education and other areas for which they have responsibility (such as health and earlier stages of education). This explicitly involves making different choices about how to spend general taxpayer money. For instance, between 2010/11 and 2013/14 Wales chose to cut the health budget by

---

[8] Formally, there is a fee (£1,820 in 2015/16) but the Scottish government pays it for Scottish residents and for most non-UK students from the rest of the European Union.

[9] These figures refer to UK domiciled students and come from the Higher Education Statistics Agency (HESA), Table 7a, https://www.hesa.ac.uk/sfr210#tables.

over 8 per cent in real terms, while health spending was ring-fenced in England.[10]

Another way to look at the choice that has been made for England is to ask what would be the additional cost to the public purse of abolishing all fees and hence following the current policy in Scotland, making university 'free'. This calculation needs to take into account the 'RAB charge' referred to above. That is, the additional expenditure required to provide 'free' university education would be less than the total sum of the loans for fees currently provided to students, because at least some of these loans will be repaid in future. We ignore the important presentational issue that neither the loans made to students nor the expected future write-offs formally count towards public spending in the UK National Accounts. We estimate, very roughly, that around an additional £6.7 billion per year would be needed if the government were to abolish tuition fees in England.[11] If the government did not want to raise taxes to pay for this, it would have to reduce expenditure elsewhere. The sum involved represents about 6 per cent of all spending on the National Health Service or about a quarter of the defence budget. Alternatively, if taxation were to be increased, it could be achieved by a rise in the basic rate of VAT from 20 per cent to 21 per cent or by increasing the revenue from corporation tax by a quarter.[12] Those arguing for a return to 'free' higher education would have to decide which of these sorts of choices should be made to finance that change.

What about elsewhere in the world? The numbers of young people going to university have increased everywhere. How have other countries coped with the cost? The OECD notes that its members 'differ dramatically in the way the cost of higher education is shared among governments, students and their families . . . and in the financial support they provide to students'.[13] This is matched by some sharp variation within countries, defying efforts at easy summary. But the position of the UK, and especially England, compared to other countries can be told quite simply. (We do not try to take account of differences between

---

[10] Deaner, B. and Phillips, D. (2013), *Scenarios for the Welsh Government Budget to 2025–26*, IFS Report 83, London: Institute for Fiscal Studies.

[11] This figure is estimated by calculating how much fee income the government would have to give universities to cover all fees for a given cohort of students minus the amount we estimate they are likely to spend subsidizing fee loans for that cohort (estimated by assuming that maintenance loans are repaid first, followed by fee loans). It assumes that the cap on tuition fees and the number of students going to university both remain fixed.

[12] Figures for current revenue raised by different taxes are taken from Office for Budget Responsibility (2015) *A Brief Guide to the UK Public Finances*, November. In making our illustrative calculations, we have ignored the changes in the behaviour of individuals and firms that would be expected with the new tax rates.

[13] OECD (2013), *Education at a Glance*, Paris: OECD, p. 228.

countries in the quality of higher education that would justify differences in fees.)

The OECD's review, published in 2013, focused on academic year 2010/11, after the 2006 fee increase in England but before the much larger rise in 2012. At this time, the UK as a whole was classified by the OECD as belonging to the group of countries with high tuition fees but well developed systems of student support, along with Australia, Canada, the Netherlands, New Zealand, and the USA. Average fees for full-time undergraduate study in public universities were reported as about 10 per cent less in the UK than in the USA (where fees for private universities, including the famous 'Ivy League' group, are far higher), about 15 per cent higher than in Canada, about 25–35 per cent higher than in Australia and New Zealand, and about two and a half times the figure in the Netherlands. The level of the much higher 2012 fees in England would easily have put the UK at the top of the table with the highest fees among the 25 countries for which the OECD collected data.[14]

A key feature of the system for student support for the costs of meeting fees (but not living costs) in Australia is a system of 'income contingent' loans, analogous to that in England. (We noted in Chapter 2 that Australia was the first country to introduce this sort of loan system for higher education.) A notable difference in Australia, compared to England, is that loans are written-off only at death. In contrast, the USA, for example, has well-developed 'mortgage-style' loan schemes for university study—loans with no write-off and a fixed repayment amount per month—together with other forms of support which vary from state to state.[15]

With the exception of the Netherlands, all European countries for which the OECD collected data were classified in 2010/11 as having 'no or low tuition fees'. These include the Nordic countries, none of which charge any tuition fees, something that the OECD describes as 'a salient feature of their culture of education'. Some of this group have well-developed systems of support for students' living costs—again the Nordic countries—but some provide little support. A more recent review by the European Union fills in the data gaps and updates the picture for

---

[14] This is confirmed in the latest figures, which are for 2013/14, given in OECD (2015), *Education at a Glance*, Paris: OECD. Our comparison of fees is based on OECD (2013), ibid., Table B5.1. It is unclear whether or not the average fee in the USA includes two year 'associate degree' courses in community colleges, which would substantially reduce the figure.

[15] The US system of providing aid to university students is reviewed in Avery, C. and Turner, S. (2012), 'Student Loans: Do College Students Borrow Too Much—Or Not Enough?' *Journal of Economic Perspectives*, 26(1): 165–92, and Dynarski, S. and Scott-Clayton, J. (2013), 'Financial aid policy: Lessons from research', *The Future of Children*, 23(1): 67–91.

other countries.[16] 'Low fee' countries include Italy and Spain, where the most common fee for 2014/15 was about £1,000 per year. Ireland has higher fees, around £2,500 being reported as the most common fee for 2014/15, but still nowhere near the level in England after 2012. Examples of other countries with negligible or zero fees include both France and Germany. In Germany, nearly half of the states, the *Länder*, had introduced tuition fees in 2007 of typically €1,000 a year following a change in federal law permitting this, but by 2014/15 they had all stopped doing so.

We have focused in this brief account on fees rather than support for living costs. Where countries offer little of the latter, students from families with low incomes may be obliged to go to the local university. In Italy, around three-quarters of undergraduate students live with their parents and about half do so in Spain.[17] Around 40 per cent are reported as living with parents in France and Ireland. We noted earlier that the great majority of undergraduate students in England live away from home. Trying to enable a wide choice of universities to which young people can realistically apply may be seen as part of the 'salient culture' of UK higher education. The next section describes arrangements in England in more detail.

In summary, England *is* therefore clearly different. Successive governments have chosen to shift an increasing amount of the burden of funding university teaching onto those who go to university. This is a choice that many European governments have not made. Fees in England are now very high by international standards. But, unique in western Europe, there is a system of 'income-contingent' loans to ensure that neither students nor their families have to pay these fees up-front and that debts are eventually written off if they cannot be paid—as is expected in many cases. There is also good support for living costs compared to many countries, through the same loan system. Whether 'good' means 'good enough' is discussed below.

Student Support Varies with Family Income

We now delve a little more into the system in England as it stands in 2016. We still abstract from some of the gory details but we do need to

[16] Eurydice (2014), *National Student Fee and Support Systems in European Higher Education 2014/15*, Brussels: The European Commission.

[17] Orr, D., Gwosc, C., and Netz, N. (2011), *Social and Economic Conditions of Student Life in Europe. Synopsis of indicators. Final report. Eurostudent IV 2008–2011*. Bielefeld: W. Bertelsmann Verlag.

Table 3.1. Fees, support for students and loan repayment terms for graduates—England, 2004–16

Element	For students starting university pre-2006	For students starting university 2006–11	For students starting university 2012–15	For students starting university in 2016
Fees	£1,200 (in 2005/6)	Max £3,375 (in 2011/12)	Max £9,000	Max £9,000
	Up front	Deferred via fee loan	Deferred via fee loan	Deferred via fee loan
	Exemptions for poorest students	No exemptions	Partial fee waivers for poorest students	Partial fee waivers for poorest students
Maintenance grants	No grants before 2004/5, £1,000 in 2005/6	Up to £2,906 (in 2011/12)	Up to £3,250 (in 2012/13)	No grants
Maintenance loans	Up to £4,195 (in 2005/6)	Up to £4,950 (in 2011/12)	Up to £5,500 (in 2012/13)	Up to £8,200 (in 2016/17)
Loan repayment	9% of income above £10,000	9% of income above £15,000 (in 2006) (uprated with RPI)	9% of income above £21,000 (in 2016) (frozen until 2021, then uprated with earnings)	9% of income above £21,000 (in 2016) (frozen until 2021 then uprated with earnings)
	Interest rate = RPI + 0%	Interest rate = RPI + 0%	Interest rate = RPI + 3% while studying, then RPI + 0% for those with income <£21,000 p.a., rising to RPI + 3% for income £41,000 +	Interest rate = RPI + 3% while studying, then RPI + 0% for those with income <£21,000 p.a., rising to RPI + 3% for income £41,000 +
	No write-off	Debt written off after 25 years	Debt written off after 30 years	Debt written off after 30 years

Notes: amounts of fees, grants, loans, and earnings are nominal annual figures. Fees before 2006 were the same for all courses and institutions. The repayment threshold for students starting university from 2012 was originally intended to be uprated with earnings from 2016. This was changed retrospectively in the 2015 Autumn Statement/Spending Review. The maximum figures for maintenance loans are for students at universities outside of London and living away from home.

describe further the changes that have been made in recent years as a prelude to looking at data on levels of applications and entry to university in Chapter 4.

Table 3.1 summarizes university fees, financial support given to students, and the repayment regime faced by graduates. The first two columns show the system immediately before the 2006 reforms and the system following the major changes in that year. The final two columns summarize the system following the 2012 reforms, and the one that, at the time of writing in early 2016, we expect to be in place for the cohort of English students entering higher education in September 2016.

What support is offered to students to cope with the expenses of going to university? We start with the costs of tuition, the focus of most of the popular debate in recent years. The key help since 2006 is common to students of all backgrounds, irrespective of family income: the fees have to be paid only after graduation. Since 2012, some students from poorer families have been offered partial fee waivers by their universities—reducing the amount they have to borrow from the government to cover their fees—although this is becoming less common. And some have received aid in the form of cash bursaries from universities, which, since 2012, have formed one element of the package of support that universities must offer as part of the requirement imposed by the Office for Fair Access to allow them to charge fees that exceed £6,000—as they have all chosen to do.

The extent of this support and how it varies across universities is limited and hard to summarize.[18] Moreover, there needs to be adequate information about the support that each university offers *before* the point at which students make their decisions on applications to university. In many cases this has not happened, with students only being told about their entitlement after the event. Unless appropriate information is made clear in advance, the support provided by universities cannot be expected to have much impact on young people's decisions to go on to higher education.

What about help to cover living costs? Unlike the fees, which are entirely deferred, the costs of living while at university have to be met up-front. We have noted that financial support for living costs is a key element of the UK system of higher education finance, providing students with a wider choice of university. As was the case with tuition fees, this element of the system has undergone substantial reform over the last fifty years as well. When small numbers of students went to university, those from poorer backgrounds received grants to help meet their

---

[18] The position in 2014 was described in Dearden, L., Hodge, L., Jin, W., Levine, A., and Williams, L. (2014), 'Financial support for HE students since 2012', IFS Briefing Note 152, London: Institute for Fiscal Studies. An analysis of bursaries received by cohorts of students entering university between 2006/7 and 2011/12 is made in Wyness, G. (2015), 'Deserving poor? Are higher education bursaries going to the right students?' Department of Quantitative Social Science Working Paper 15-09, UCL Institute of Education. Wyness finds large differences in the amount of aid received among poor students but that the brightest, poorest students do tend to receive the most bursary aid.

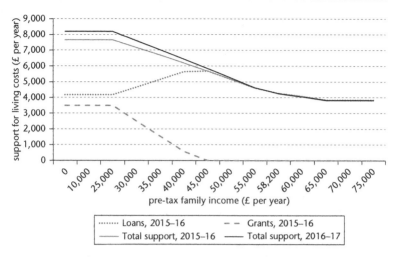

Figure 3.2. Grant and loan support to cover students' living costs before and after abolition of maintenance grants, by level of gross annual family income

Note: Total support in 2016–17 is comprised entirely of loans. The graph shows the situation for a student living away from home attending a university outside London. The 2015–16 figures show the support we would have expected students to receive in 2016–17 had grants not been replaced by loans. (Specifically, we assume that the amounts received would have been uprated in line with the Retail Prices Index, but that the family income thresholds would have been fixed in nominal terms.) All figures are in 2016 prices.

Source: Britton, J., Crawford, C., and Dearden, L. (2015), 'Analysis of the higher education funding reforms announced in the summer budget', Institute for Fiscal Studies Briefing Note BN174, London.

living expenses.[19] The generosity of these grants fell over time, and they were eventually partially and then fully replaced by maintenance loans in the early 2000s. When tuition fees were announced to be increasing in 2006, maintenance grants were re-introduced for the poorest students, with their value roughly increasing in line with inflation up to 2015. From 2016, they have been abolished again, however, and replaced by slightly larger maintenance loans.

Figure 3.2 shows how the total amount and composition of financial support that students receive from the government varies with family income, before and after the 2016 reforms (in 2016 prices). The graph shows the situation for a student resident in England who lives away from home and who is studying at a university outside London.

---

[19] See Wilson, W. (1997), 'Student grants, loans and tuition fees', House of Commons Library Research Paper 97/119.

Until 2015, a student from a family with pre-tax family income below £25,000 per year would have received the full maintenance grant and about 70 per cent of the maximum maintenance loan, providing a total of about £7,650 per year. Support then fell as family income rose. The grant was extinguished when gross family income reached £43,000 per year. The maintenance loan fell to a minimum level of about £3,800 per year when gross family income exceeded £62,000 per year.

From 2016, similar variation in total support by family income remains, but the composition of that support is now completely different for those with family incomes below £43,000 per year. While the total support available has increased slightly for these students—to around £8,200 per year—it is now offered entirely in the form of loans that have to be repaid after graduation; maintenance grants have been abolished.

It is important to emphasize that the key thresholds of family income which determine the different levels of support shown in Figure 3.2 are set at levels that result in large numbers of students qualifying for more support than the minimum on offer. Figures from the Student Loans Company—the body which manages student loans on behalf of the government—show that 41 per cent of individuals claimed the full maintenance grant in 2014/15, while another 14 per cent claimed a partial grant.[20] All these individuals would now get loans under the arrangements in place from 2016, rather than grants, but the loans would be above the minimum level. Loans greater than the minimum amount will also be received by those individuals with family pre-tax income above the old threshold for any grant payment but below the threshold of about £65,000 at which only the minimum loan is paid. The system therefore offers substantial support of over £5,000 per year to a large fraction of students and some support to all students. A maintenance loan for living costs, albeit at a lower level (a maximum of £6,900 in 2014/15), is offered even if the student is living with their parents—in contrast to the situation in many other countries.

Is the level of support adequate, especially for students from poorer families? We looked at data on undergraduate student expenditure in England from the most recent government-sponsored survey, which is for 2011/12. Average living costs for young full-time students outside London and not living at home were £8,700 for the nine months of the academic year. This figure is the median, so half of students spent more than this amount and half less. About 80 per cent of students had

---

[20] 'Student Support for Higher Education in England, Academic Year 2014–15 (Provisional)', Student Loans Company Statistical First Release 05/2014.

expenditure that was above the maximum amount of the maintenance loan and grant of around £6,400 available in 2011/12. The National Union of Students (NUS) reports a substantially higher estimate of average costs for 2012/13 of around £12,000 outside London, well above the maximum support provided by loans and grants. The NUS website warns students that, in the union's view, they may need 'several thousand pounds a year' from other sources to cover the shortfall. Indeed, many prospective students report that they are likely to work both during and outside term-time while they are at university, and an increasing proportion are electing to live at home or go to a university closer to home.[21] On the other hand, the UK Border Agency requires applicants for a student visa to demonstrate that they have £820 a month if they are studying outside London. This equates broadly to the maximum level of support offered to English students through loans and, until 2016, grants, which may be no coincidence.[22]

Another possible yardstick is what a young person would earn over nine months if working full-time at the national minimum wage for 18–20 year olds. The answer for 2015/16 was about £7,700, before deductions (this figure was below the income tax threshold and National Insurance contributions would have been very modest). On this basis, the maximum support for students' living costs appears very similar to the amount the government guarantees to people of the same age if they work.

It is clear that student funding is far from being so generous that young people from poorer families are able to afford to go to university with ease. Students from families on middle or higher incomes will clearly lack all the resources they need unless parents make up the difference. But whether lack of funding for living costs is a substantial barrier in practice, reducing the numbers that would otherwise go to university, is another matter. Chapter 4 considers whether the changes to tuition fees and student support that have been introduced over the last few years have detrimentally affected the numbers of

[21] Atherton, G., Jones, S., and Hall, A. (2015), *Does Cost Matter? Students' understanding of the higher education finance system and how cost affects their decisions*, National Education Opportunities Network Report.

[22] Our calculations using the Student Income and Expenditure Survey data for 2011/12 relate to students aged under 25 and exclude tuition fees and other 'participation costs' (e.g. books). For further details of the survey, see Department for Business, Innovation and Skills (2013), *Student Income and Expenditure Survey 2011/12*; NUS estimates come from 'What are the costs of study and living?' on http://www.nus.org.uk; visa requirements are from UK Visas and Immigration (2014), *Guide to Supporting Documents: Points based System—Tier 4 (General)*.

young people—especially those from poorer backgrounds—who choose to go to university.

Repayment Varies Greatly with Lifetime Income

While one benefit of the system in England is that fees do not have to be paid up-front, the flipside is that most students now leave university with significant levels of debt. How big will the debt be? We estimate that students entering university in 2016/17 will graduate with debts from their fee and maintenance loans averaging nearly £50,000 (in 2016 prices).[23] (They may also have other debts, for example from use of credit cards, which we do not consider.) The size of this figure leads to the sorts of newspaper headlines mentioned at the start of the chapter. Fee debt does not vary much by family income, but since maintenance grants were replaced by slightly larger maintenance loans in 2016, students from the poorest families are entitled to the largest mainten-ance loans. These students are therefore estimated to graduate with the largest debts—of more than £53,000 if they take out the full amount of loans to which they are entitled—see Figure 3.3. This was not the case in 2015, when it was students from middle income families who qualified for the largest maintenance loans (students from poorer families having grants and, as a result, lower loans) and hence graduated with the largest debts.

This fee and maintenance debt is not like ordinary debt, however. The terms of repayment are summarized in Table 3.1. In essence, graduates must repay a percentage of their income above a given threshold once their income reaches that threshold. They make repayments until the loan is paid off, or until the fixed maximum repayment period ends, whichever comes sooner. Any outstanding debt left at the end of this repayment period is written off.

For those entering university before 2012, graduates repaid 9 per cent of their income above £17,846 (in 2016 prices) for a maximum of 25 years, and the size of their loan increased in line with price inflation. For those entering university after 2012, graduates still have to repay 9 per cent of income in excess of a threshold but the threshold has risen to £21,000 (in 2016 prices). In late 2015, the government announced

---

[23] Britton, J., Crawford, C., and Dearden, L. (2015), 'Analysis of the higher education funding reforms announced in the summer budget', IFS Briefing Note BN174, London: Institute for Fiscal Studies.

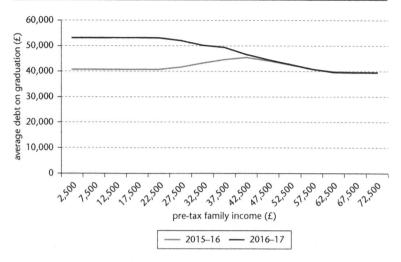

Figure 3.3. Estimates of average student debt on graduation before and after abolition of maintenance grants, by level of gross annual family income

Note: These figures are estimated for young English-domiciled students entering one of the 90 largest universities in England to study full-time in 2016–17. We assume that all students take out the full fee and maintenance loans to which they are entitled and that there is no dropout from university. The 2015–16 figures are what we would have expected for students entering university in 2016–17 had maintenance grants not been replaced by loans. (Specifically we assume that the available maintenance loan amounts would have been uprated in line with the Retail Prices Index, but that the family income thresholds would have been fixed in nominal terms. We also assume that fees would have been fixed in nominal terms from 2015–16 onwards. This is reasonable, as most universities were already charging the maximum £9,000 fee in 2015–16.) All figures are in 2016 prices.

Source: Britton, J., Crawford, C., and Dearden, L. (2015), 'Analysis of the higher education funding reforms announced in the summer budget', Institute for Fiscal Studies Briefing Note BN174, London.

that this threshold will be frozen in cash terms for five years. The expectation is that it will rise in line with average earnings thereafter.

These changes reduce both the number of graduates who have to make repayments each year, and, for those who have to make repayments, the amount they repay each year, compared to the situation pre-2012. On the other hand, repayments now have to be made for a longer time, for up to 30 years. And students are also charged a 'real' interest rate of 3 per cent while they are studying—that is, a rate 3 per cent above the rate of inflation—and of between 0 per cent and 3 per cent once they are liable for repayments, the top rate applying when income reaches £41,000 per year.

These changes increase the debt and reduce annual repayments, hence the period over which graduates have to make repayments has

increased significantly for many. Under the system in place up to 2011/
12, we estimate that nearly half of graduates would have repaid
their debt in full by the age of 40. Only a very small fraction—about
7 per cent—are likely to achieve that under the 2016 system. But,
remarkably, because of the higher income threshold and the finite period
over which repayment is made—albeit a longer period than before—we
expect that almost 70 per cent of graduates will not pay back their loans
in full. Graduates are expected to pay back *more* on average in absolute
terms but *less* as a percentage of their total, now higher, debt.

We have been careful to use the word 'estimate' when referring to
amounts of debt and repayment. The amount of debt varies across
students, depending on their choice of university and subject (which
determines the precise fee level and length of course), their family
income (which determines the maintenance loan to which they are
entitled) and their other characteristics such as prior attainment
(which, together with their family income and the university they
attend, determines any fee waivers they will be offered). We have to
allow for this variation in order to judge the impact of the reforms on
the average amount of debt with which graduates leave university. The
figures we produce are our best estimates based on a set of assumptions.

We also have to make a series of assumptions to come up with our
estimates for the average amount of debt that will eventually be repaid
and of how many graduates will never repay all their debt. Our figures
are based on detailed modelling by some of us for a simulated cohort of
young people assumed to enter full-time higher education in September
2012. We predict how much these graduates are likely to earn in each
year throughout their working lives based on what has been established
from other data sources about how individuals' earnings change from
year to year, adjusted for official forecasts of future average earnings
growth.[24] Based on these earnings profiles, we estimate how much we
would expect graduates to repay each year and in total, assuming perfect
compliance.

How much we estimate graduates will have to repay depends on how
much we estimate they will earn and what we assume about the loan
repayment terms that they face. Our figures in this part of the chapter
use earnings growth forecasts from the independent Office for Budget

---

[24] In principle, graduates must make student loan repayments out of unearned income
exceeding £2,000 per year. In practice, however, only those who submit self-assessment tax
returns make repayments on the basis of unearned income. The number of individuals to
whom this applies is small, so earnings and income can be regarded as synonymous in this
context.

Responsibility, and assume that the parameters of the loan system remain unchanged.[25] Due to the cumulative effect of average earnings growth over the thirty-year repayment period, our estimates are sensitive to changes in these forecasts.

As we outlined earlier, when estimating the cost of student loans to the government, it is not only the loan repayment terms and estimated graduate incomes that affect these estimates, but also how highly the government values these expected future repayments today. This depends on how much it costs them to borrow the money to lend to students, and how much they value the alternative uses to which that money could have been put. These judgements are captured using something called a 'discount rate'. This tells us how much less valuable the government regards money tomorrow compared to money today: the higher the discount rate, the less it values money tomorrow, i.e. the less it values the student loan repayments it expects to receive in future.

While this valuation does not affect how much money the government expects to receive in future, it does affect the 'RAB charge' that we mentioned earlier. Indeed estimates of how much of each £1 lent to students is likely to be repaid in future are very sensitive to the assumption made about the appropriate discount rate. In late 2015, the government announced that it would reduce the discount rate applied to student loans from 2.2 per cent above the rate of inflation to 0.7 per cent above the rate of inflation, to reflect the fact that the current cost of government borrowing is relatively low. This change is important from a presentational perspective: with the higher discount rate, we estimate the RAB charge to be 38 per cent for the cohort of students who entered university in 2012, while with the lower discount rate we estimate it to be 18 per cent. Thus, while changing the discount rate does not affect the real repayments that graduates are estimated to make in future, it steers the public debate in a rather unhelpful way via its effect on the RAB charge, which has been incorrectly characterized as a way of capturing the 'sustainability' of the student loan system.

Notwithstanding these concerns about the uncertainty of the overall cost to government and graduates of a university education, it is nonetheless helpful to compare the variation in expected graduate repayments based on a given set of assumptions. This helps us to understand how progressive is the loan repayment system. Figure 3.4 shows our estimates of how loan repayments vary across the distribution of graduate

---

[25] Details of the methodology are given in Crawford, C., Crawford, R., and Jin, W. (2014), *Estimating the public cost of student loans*, IFS Report No. 94, London: Institute for Fiscal Studies.

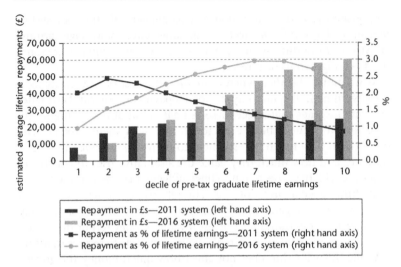

Figure 3.4. Estimates of total debt repayments in £s and as a % of lifetime earnings across the distribution of graduate lifetime earnings

Note: The amounts of debt and of earnings are 'net present value' figures, meaning that they are the sum (in 2015 prices) of the value of future streams of debt repayment and earnings over the 30-year loan repayment term, taking account of the fact that money in future is less valuable now than money in your pocket today. The amount shown for each decile group is the average figure for graduates in that part of the distribution of pre-tax lifetime earnings.

Source: Authors' calculations using the Institute for Fiscal Studies' graduate repayments model. See Crawford, C., Crawford, R., and Jin, W. (2014), *Estimating the public cost of student loans*, Institute for Fiscal Studies Report R94, for a description of this model and Britton, J., Crawford, C., and Dearden, L. (2015), 'Analysis of the higher education funding reforms announced in the summer budget', IFS Briefing Note BN174, London: Institute for Fiscal Studies for further updates on the parameters used.

lifetime earnings. The graph splits our simulated cohort of graduates into ten equally-sized groups on the basis of the earnings we estimate they would receive across their working lives. The two bars for each group show graduates' expected average total repayments across their working lives in today's money (i.e. after having applied a discount rate of 0.7 per cent above the rate of inflation) under the system operating before 2012 and following the 2016 reforms (left-hand axis). The two lines show the average total repayments as a percentage of lifetime income (right-hand axis).

The graph shows that the 2016 system is much more progressive than the 2011 system. That is, the positive relationship between the amount of repayments and lifetime earnings has become stronger: following the 2012 and 2016 reforms, the bars rise much more steeply as one moves from left to right in the diagram. For example, the 10 per cent lowest-earning graduates are only estimated to repay around £4,000 in total in today's money under the 2016 system, compared with around £8,000 in total in today's money under the 2011 system. In fact, the 25 per cent lowest-earning graduates, whose income rarely exceeds the new higher threshold of £21,000 per year, are estimated to repay less in total in today's money than they did under the pre-2012 system. At the other end of the distribution, repayments are expected to more than double among some of the highest earning graduates. These graduates are estimated to have to pay back all of their debt.

The progressivity of the new system can also be judged by the lines showing total repayments in today's money as a percentage of lifetime income. Under the 2011 system, individuals in the bottom half of the total gross graduate lifetime earnings distribution repaid more as a percentage of their lifetime earnings than individuals in the top half of the graduate lifetime earnings distribution, while the opposite is true under the 2016 system. It is also worth noting that the percentages of lifetime earnings that graduates spend repaying their student loans are small compared with the estimates we reported in Chapter 1 for the average lifetime increase in earnings as the result of going to university (of around 25 per cent). These figures are also very small compared to the best estimates of median lifetime average tax rates for the UK, which are just under 25 per cent for the highest-earning 30 per cent of individuals.[26]

Summing Up

Undergraduate tuition fees charged by universities in England have risen substantially since 2011. They are now very high by international standards but the support offered to students in the form of 'income contingent' loans—to cover both fees and living costs—is good compared to that in other countries. These loans provide an insurance system, ensuring that those who end up doing worst in the labour market pay back the least (and often much less than they borrow in today's money). This means that the risk of undertaking a degree is relatively low despite the high tuition fees that are charged. Chapter 4 investigates whether concerns about the rising costs of going to university have reduced the numbers of young people—especially those from poorer backgrounds—who decide to go.

[26] See Brewer, M., Costa Dias, M., and Shaw, J. (2012), 'Lifetime inequality and redistribution', IFS Working Paper W12/23, London: Institute for Fiscal Studies.

4

Have Recent Funding Reforms Widened the Family Background Gaps?

This chapter studies the changes that have taken place in recent years in terms of applications and entry to university in England. Of particular interest is whether the reforms to higher education funding and arrangements for student support described in the last chapter have affected university applications and entry, particularly amongst young people from lower socio-economic backgrounds. How have the family background gaps changed in practice over a period in which tuition fees roughly trebled (between 2005 and 2006), and then roughly trebled again (between 2011 and 2012)? The measures of family background in the available data are not ideal, as we explain later in the chapter, but they are sufficient for the purpose. The raw data suggest that, if anything, the gaps in both applications and entrance have narrowed as fees have increased.

How have Family Background Gaps Changed in Recent Years?

We have explained how the fees, the financial support provided during study, and the rules governing the eventual repayment of debts, have changed in recent years. But the proof of the pudding is in the eating. How have application and entry to university by young people actually changed in England? Does behaviour appear to have been affected much in practice? A key concern associated with the changes in the funding of higher education in 2006 and in 2012 was whether they would put people off from going to university—especially those from the poorest backgrounds.

Looking at trends in the numbers of individuals applying to and attending university, these concerns do not appear to have been realized, at least as far as young applicants for full-time study are concerned, the group we are focusing on in this book. (We refer very briefly to part-time applicants towards the end of the chapter.) We should stress that this is not 'hard' evidence of the type really needed though. It is only 'soft' evidence, as it simply shows the situation before and after the changes in fees and support. But other factors may also have been at work that changed the behaviour of young people and universities over the period in question. What we see in the graphs will reflect the influence of these factors as well as the changes in the funding system. We return to this problem later.

The graphs are all based on tabulated data from the university admissions service, UCAS. The information available on family background is limited. We use two measures. First, the data record whether or not an individual received free school meals when they were aged 15. This is a very commonly used indicator of low family income but it is a far from perfect guide to poverty. Second, UCAS splits young people into five equal sized groups according to the past rate of entry to higher education in their local area (over the years 2000 to 2004). Areas with high past entry rates have a higher concentration of richer, more educated, or 'advantaged' families and areas with low past entry rates have more poorer, less educated, or 'disadvantaged' families.

Figure 4.1 shows the percentage of eighteen-year-olds in England who entered university in each year between 2007 and 2014. Like our other graphs, it refers to entry to a university anywhere in the UK. The graph distinguishes between those individuals who received free school meals and those who did not. There was a substantial rise in the entry rate across these years for both groups, from 10 per cent to 15 per cent and from 25 per cent to 30 per cent respectively, with the difference in entry rates between the two groups unchanged. The introduction of the maximum £9,000 fees in 2012 does not seem to have been associated with a clear shift for either group (we return to the apparent 'blip' in 2011 below).

But we need to dig further. We can look at the changes over a slightly longer period, starting in 2004. This spans the 2006 reforms as well. And now we include young people who went to private schools, who were excluded from Figure 4.1. The available data mean we have to switch to the second measure of family background based on past entry rates to higher education in each individual's local area. Figure 4.2 shows that entry rates have risen the most amongst young people from the *least* advantaged areas, from 10 per cent in 2004 to 18 per cent in 2014, compared to the rise from 43 per cent to 46 per cent for the most

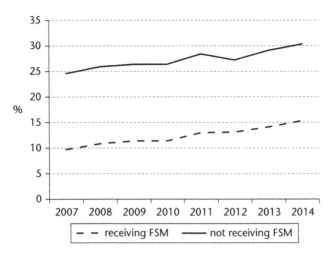

Figure 4.1. 18-year-olds in England entering university (%), by whether they received free school meals (FSM), 2007–14

Note: Young people who went to state schools only. Free school meals receipt is at age 15.

Source: *UCAS End of Cycle Report 2014*, Figure 82.

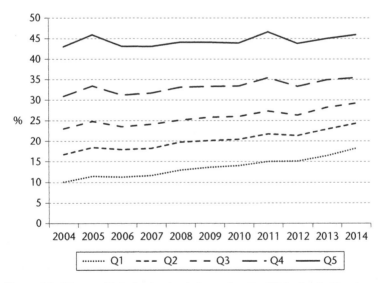

Figure 4.2. 18-year-olds in England entering university (%), by level of local area 'disadvantage', 2004–14

Note: Q1 is the most disadvantaged group; Q5 is the least disadvantaged. See the text for further explanation.

Source: *UCAS End of Cycle Report 2014*, Figure 74 (2006 onwards) and 2013 Report, Figure 56 (2004–5, adjusted by ratio of 2006 figures in 2014 report to those in 2013 report).

advantaged group. The difference between these two groups has there-fore fallen—there has been some catch-up among the least advantaged young people.

There does not seem to have been a notable downward shift in entry rates for any of the five groups around the time of the 2006 reforms or those of 2012. However, in both cases there was an upward 'blip' in the year preceding the change followed by a fall, especially for the more advantaged groups. This may have been due to eighteen-year-olds forgoing a 'gap year' that they would otherwise have taken and going to university a year earlier than planned in order to avoid the fee changes, which were announced well in advance. This is one reason why it is useful to consider rates of entry to university at either age 18 or age 19 for 'cohorts' of young people as they finish secondary schooling—see Figure 4.3, which spans 2007 to 2013.[1] These cohort entry rates are

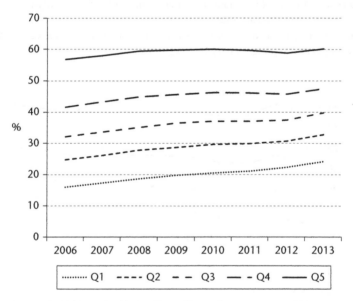

Figure 4.3. Share of age cohort in England entering university (%) at either age 18 or 19, by level of local area 'disadvantage', 2007–13

Note: the year on the horizontal axis is that in which the cohort reached the age of 18. Q1 is the most disadvantaged group; Q5 is the least disadvantaged. See the text for further explanation.

Source: UCAS End of Cycle Report 2014, Figure 75.

[1] These are the years when the young people in each cohort could first enter university, so the figures for 2013, for example, are the rates of entry in either 2013 at age 18 or in 2014 at age 19 for young people becoming 18 in 2013.

higher than those shown in Figures 4.1 and 4.2 as they include all young people entering at either age. The switch in definition increases the difference in entry rates in any given year between young people from more advantaged and less advantaged local areas. This is because taking a gap year and going to university at age 19 is more common for teenagers from higher socio-economic backgrounds, and the age 19 entrants were excluded from Figures 4.1 and 4.2. But the story of the changes over the period is the same, and the gap in entry rates between the most and least advantaged groups again falls, from 41 percentage points in 2007 to 36 points in 2013.

Up to this point we have not distinguished between entry to higher status and lower status universities. Tuition fees do vary modestly across different universities, and may be more likely to do so in future if government plans to vary fees with teaching quality are realized. (At the end of 2015, the government announced its intention to allow institutions with excellent teaching to raise fees in line with inflation each year.[2]) It is possible that a higher cost of university might lead to more young people from less advantaged backgrounds going to universities that charge lower fees. Is there any evidence that suggests this has happened? Figure 4.4 shows entry rates to 'higher tariff' universities, distinguishing between young people in the least advantaged and the most advantaged groups, using the same definition of disadvantage based on local area as in Figures 4.2 and 4.3. 'Higher tariff' universities are those whose recent student intakes have had the highest average A-level achievement. About a third of eighteen-year-olds studying for a degree in the UK are at these universities. Figure 4.4 plots the entry rate for eighteen-year-olds to higher tariff universities among young people resident in England from the least advantaged areas on the left hand axis. These rates are very low—only in 2014 do they even reach 3 per cent. The rate for the most advantaged areas is plotted on the right hand axis. (Both axes have the same range—four percentage points.) These are far higher—the figure is around 20 per cent in every year.

The large difference comes as no surprise, reflecting the pattern of entry to universities of different status that we highlighted in Chapter 1. But the key point here is that there is no marked drop in entry rates for the least advantaged group around the time of the 2012 reforms. Indeed, their highest rate comes after 2012 (although it should be noted that the differences from year to year are very small). This also suggests, however,

---

[2] In Autumn 2015, the government launched a consultation on the future of higher education: 'Fulfilling our Potential: Teaching Excellence, Social Mobility and Student Choice', Cm 9141.

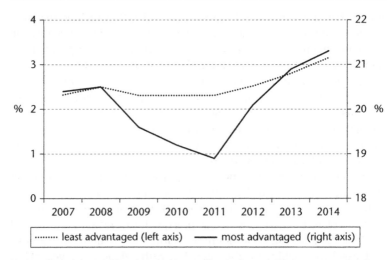

Figure 4.4. 18-year-olds in England entering 'higher tariff' universities (%), least advantaged areas and most advantaged areas, 2007–14

Note: See the text for further explanation of least and most advantaged.

Source: UCAS End of Cycle Report 2014, Figures 76 and 77.

that the main explanation for the rise in entry to any type of university for the least advantaged eighteen-year-olds shown earlier in Figure 4.2 has been an increase in their entry to 'lower tariff' universities—those with the least well qualified students on average in terms of secondary school qualifications. Given that the benefits of going to university are higher at higher-tariff universities, as we described in Chapter 1, this suggests that the narrowing of the gap in participation may not be fully mirrored by a reduction in earnings inequality after graduation.

Our final issue is the distinction between applications and entry. Our graphs so far have focused on entry. But not all applicants to universities get offers. And it is applications that best reflect the demand for higher education. By looking at applications we can also take the story one year further on. Figure 4.5 shows the percentage of eighteen-year-olds in England making applications to any UK university between 2007 and 2015, distinguishing as before between young people from the least advantaged areas and the most advantaged areas.[3] (In this graph, young

---

[3] The graph uses data for applications made by eighteen-year-olds for entry in September 2015 (or for entry in 2016 following a 'gap year') by the time of a standard January deadline that features prominently in the annual cycle. UCAS reports that 'typically 97 per cent . . . of 18 year old UK domiciled applicants' make their applications by the January deadline (UCAS

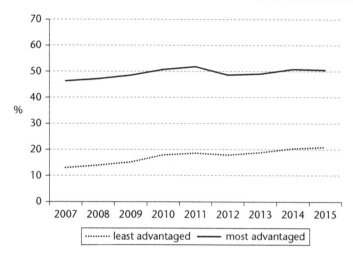

Figure 4.5. 18-year-olds in England applying to university (%), least advantaged areas and most advantaged areas, 2007–15

Note: See the text for further explanation of least and most advantaged.

Source: UCAS (2015), *UK application rates by country, region, constituency, sex, age and background (January deadline, 2015 cycle)*, Figures 15 and 16.

people are classified according to entry rates in their local area between 2005 and 2009 rather than between 2000 and 2004 as in earlier graphs.) Application rates amongst prospective students from the least advantaged areas rise across the period from 13 per cent to 21 per cent, compared to an increase from 46 per cent to 51 per cent for the most advantaged areas. There is a steeper rise for the less advantaged, showing the same clear catch-up as we noted earlier for entry. And there is again no obvious evidence of a marked shift in the trend in application rates following the 2012 reforms for this least advantaged group. For eighteen-year-olds from the most advantaged areas there does appear to have been a flattening off, with applications in 2015 at the same level as in 2010, before the 'blip' again evident in the data for 2011.

Other Evidence?

We stress again that our analysis provides only 'soft' evidence of the potential effect of changes to the cost of university on higher education

(2015), *UK application rates by country, region, constituency, sex, age and background (January deadline, 2015 cycle)*, Cheltenham: UCAS, p. 6).

participation rates. We have simply looked at how entry and applications have changed between 2004 and 2015—a period when other things have occurred that may also have affected individuals' and universities' decisions on application and entry to higher education. The real effects of the 2006 and 2012 reforms alone may be disguised.

First, and most obvious, the UK experienced a large economic downturn following the global financial crisis of 2007/8. The unemployment rate for 18–24-year-olds doubled between 2004 and 2011 from about 10 per cent to 20 per cent, before easing to around 15 per cent by 2014.[4] Surely, changes in the labour market of this type influenced young people's behaviour to some extent and in ways that may have varied by family background? Some commentators talk about the impact of such changes on decisions to enter higher education as if it were straightforward—that young people can sit out a recession by going to university. But economic theory suggests that the effect of an economic downturn depends also on the view that individuals take of how long the downturn will last, on whether it is thought likely to reduce employment prospects for graduates as well, and on its impact on the incomes of parents who might contribute to the student's upkeep at university. We just don't know what have been the effects of the 'Great Recession' on choices made about going to university or not and how these choices have varied by family background.

Second, and less well known, there have been some improvements in the performance at school of teenagers from poorer backgrounds. Their achievement in public exams has seen some modest catch-up with their peers from better-off families. For example, the difference between the percentage of pupils who are and are not eligible for free school meals who achieve the government benchmark of five A*–C grades at GCSE including English and Maths fell by around 2 percentage points (from 28 to 26 percentage points) between 2005 and 2012.[5] It seems likely that this relative improvement in GCSE results may have led to some catch-up in university application and entry as well, as larger numbers of disadvantaged young people qualify for further and higher education. But the extent to which this has caused the patterns shown in the graphs, including any ironing-out of shifts in behaviour that would have been produced by the reforms to fees and funding in 2006 and 2012, is again unclear.

---

[4] Seasonally adjusted figures for the UK from series UNEM01, the Office for National Statistics website, 21 January 2015 release.

[5] See Figure 3.1 of the Social Mobility and Child Poverty Commission's *State of the Nation*, Report 2014.

Third, most of the reforms to university finance that have occurred since 1998 have combined any increase in fees with an increase in funding per student. In principle this leads to an increase in the quality of the teaching provided, better facilities for studying, or other improvements in the 'student experience' such as the campus sports facilities. All of this may influence positively the desire to go to university—if potential applicants are aware of the changes.

Fourth, during the period in question there were changes to the supply of university places through progressive relaxation of government controls on student numbers. This started in 2012/13, as noted in Chapter 3. We cannot interpret the changes in entry rates as if they were the result only of changes in demand. The final removal of any control in 2015/16 could be positive for students from poorer families. On average, they are the lower performing students in school whom we might think of as being the marginal candidates who would otherwise not have got in, although the historical perspective we took in Chapter 1 is a reminder that expansion in university provision has not closed socio-economic gaps in entry to higher education in the past.

What other evidence can be brought to bear? Some research has tried to move beyond simply *describing* what has happened to the numbers of young people going to university and has attempted to predict what would have happened in the absence of the reforms. By comparing what actually happened to what we might have expected to happen, the idea is that we can infer the effect of the reforms on entry to higher education. The difficulty here is that it is not at all easy to accurately predict what would have happened.

One possibility is to extrapolate the trends in university entry that were evident in England prior to the reforms, and to consider any deviations from these trends as evidence of the impact of the reforms. Doing so suggests that the socio-economic gap in entry did not widen as a result of the increase in the fee cap from around £1,000 per year to around £3,000 per year that took place in 2006/7.[6] But numerous other reforms took place in the early 2000s, meaning that the trend in university participation over that period may have been affected by these other changes as well.

Another possibility might be to compare what has happened in England with any changes in the applications and entry to university of young people resident in Scotland and Wales. As we have explained, these young people did not face the sharp rise in tuition fees in 2012

---

[6] Crawford, C. (2012), 'Socio-economic gaps in HE participation: How have they changed over time?' IFS Briefing Note BN133, London: Institute for Fiscal Studies.

that confronted students resident in England. Might they provide a suitable 'control group', showing what would have happened in England in the absence of the 2012 reforms? Tempting though this seems, any investigation along these lines would need to consider carefully whether Scotland and Wales really do make for an adequate comparison. For example, did the Great Recession have a different impact across the UK? Do the differences in Scotland's educational system—different secondary school qualifications, a standard four-year undergraduate degree—affect the situation? And it is questionable whether comparable data are available for each country with which to carry out such an analysis.

A further route is to look at the existing evidence on the impact of changes in university finance and student aid. What does it tell us? Much of this evidence relates to other countries, in particular the USA, where the institutional details, university culture, and other important context are not the same as in England.[7] Nevertheless, some important lessons can be found.

First, researchers have emphasized that the separate impacts of changes in fees, grants, and loans have to be considered. These impacts are usually difficult to disentangle given that reforms often involve a package of simultaneous changes. Fees may go up but if loans and grants are made more generous it is quite possible that there is little net effect. And there is also the issue of any change in quality of provision as a result of the higher fees, to which we have already referred in the UK context. Nevertheless, the evidence points to raised fees reducing university enrolment and to improvements in grants and loans increasing it.[8] Our own recent work has tried to identify the impact of changes in maintenance grants in the UK for students from low-income families and suggests that the payment of this form of support has been an important part of a strategy to reduce differences in university enrolment by family background.[9] This evidence suggests that the ending of maintenance grants from 2016 is a negative step (although we don't

[7] Some of this evidence is summarized in Department for Business, Innovation and Skills (2010), 'Review of Student Support Arrangements in Other Countries', BIS Research Paper 10.

[8] See, for example, Kane, T. (1995), 'Rising public college tuition and college entry: How well do public subsidies promote access to college?' National Bureau of Economic Research Working Paper No. 5164; Dynarski, S. (2003), 'Does aid matter? Measuring the effect of student aid on college attendance and completion', *American Economic Review*, 93: 279–88; Dynarski, S. (2008), 'Building the stock of college-educated labor', *Journal of Human Resources*, 43: 576–610.

[9] Dearden, L., Fitzsimons, E., and Wyness, G. (2014), 'Money for nothing: estimating the impact of student aid on participation in higher education', *Economics of Education Review*, 43(1): 66–78.

know to what extent students may regard the availability of slightly higher maintenance loans as suitable compensation for their loss).

Second, it is clear that the information available to young people and their families is crucial. Whether or not students, especially those from poorer backgrounds, are deterred from going to university as a result of increased fees will depend on how successful the government, universities, schools and other stakeholders are in explaining to young people the nature of the investment that higher education represents, the wages that graduates typically command, and the mechanics of any system of loans and other financial aid. The US literature emphasizes the distinction between the 'sticker price' of going to university—the headline fee—and the amount that a student actually has to pay given the support available from the government, from universities themselves and from other sources. Decisions need to be made in the light of actual prices faced and not 'sticker prices'.

There is a particular shortage of evidence on the impact of offering the 'income-contingent' loans that now play such an important role in financing higher education in England. As we have emphasized in Chapters 2 and 3, these are quite different from the 'mortgage-style' loans that prevail in the USA and to which most of the evidence on the impact of loans relates. Far too little is known about how these sorts of loans are perceived by young people and how changes in key parameters of the system—the real interest rate, the payback period, the earnings threshold for repayment—affect behaviour.

There is a range of evidence, including from England, on the views of young people towards debt, including debt that results from a decision to go to university.[10] Many young people—like other people—dislike the prospect of large debts. But it is unclear whether they fully understand the nature of the debt associated with an income-contingent loan. And an expressed dislike of debt may not, at the end of the day, actually change someone's behaviour and stop them applying to university.

In short, the 'Other evidence?' of this section is insufficient. We are unable to tell whether our simple graphs of changes in applications and entry tell the correct story of the impact of the 2006 and 2012 reforms. The prima facie evidence which the graphs provide is that the reforms—a whole package of changes in grants and loans as well as in the 'sticker price' fees—had little effect. But any firmer conclusion will have to await better research.

---

[10] See, for example, Callender, C. (2003), *Attitudes to Debt*, London: Universities UK.

It should also be noted that the conclusion of little apparent effect applies to the group we are focusing on—young applicants to full-time study. We have not considered the recent trends for part-time study where there has been a very sharp fall in student numbers: the total number of part-time UK and EU entrants (of all ages) to undergraduate study almost halved between 2010/11 and 2013/14. In this case, part of the explanation almost certainly lies with the change in fees and student support (although student numbers were falling—albeit at a slower rate—even before the reforms were introduced). This is because although income-contingent loans for fees were introduced in 2012 for part-time students, eligibility was restricted to those individuals studying for a first degree; individuals undertaking a second degree with the purpose of retraining, for example, were not entitled to a loan to cover their fees (although this restriction has now been relaxed for those studying for second degrees in science, technology, engineering or maths). More research is clearly needed to pin down the precise contribution of the funding reforms for all types of students.[11]

Summing Up

Our main aim in this chapter has been to answer the question of whether the substantial differences in university entry for full-time study by young people from different family backgrounds are caused by the costs of going to university and, in particular, whether the sharp rises in tuition fees in 2006 and 2012 have exacerbated these differences.

Whether young people from poorer backgrounds are in practice deterred from going to university as a result of higher fees probably depends on a whole range of factors: whether the fees have to be paid upfront or are covered by a loan; the type of loan system in place; whether students and their families understand the fee and loan system; the extent of grants and loans available to cover living costs and the conditions under which they are paid; whether there is unmet demand for university places at the current level of fees; and whether the increase in fees is combined with an increase in the quality of higher education on offer. We have not tried to quantify the role of each of these factors. And we have been careful to note the 'soft' nature of the evidence we

---

[11] Recent trends in part-time enrolment and possible explanations for changes are discussed in Hefce (2014), *Higher education in England 2014: Analysis of latest shifts and trends*, April 2014, 2014/08, and Callender, C. (2014), *The demise of part-time undergraduate higher education in England: Who cares?* UCL Institute of Education, London.

have considered on recent trends in applications and entry to university by young people in England. But on the face of it, the evidence does not suggest that the large rise in fees in 2012 has discouraged many young people from poorer backgrounds from going to university. The main explanation for the differences by family background in university entry lies elsewhere, as Chapter 5 explains.

5

What is the Role of Prior Attainment?

Chapter 4 showed that the repeated increases in tuition fees that England has experienced in recent decades, and the subsequent rise in the costs of going to university, have not as yet produced a decline in university enrolment, at least among young full-time students. In fact, participation in higher education has increased to the point that over a third of young people aged under twenty-one go on to university, and participation rates have been rising more rapidly amongst those from more deprived backgrounds, such that the socio-economic gap in participation has actually declined somewhat in recent years.

This does not mean, however, that we can be sanguine about the large differences in the likelihood of going to university between individuals from different socio-economic backgrounds. These are long standing and stubbornly persistent over time, despite myriad attempts by policy-makers to ensure that able students from poor backgrounds have the opportunity to go to university. Further, even among those who do go to university, students from richer backgrounds are far more likely to enrol in the higher status institutions, with long-run consequences for their careers and subsequent earnings.

So why are there such big differences in university attendance by family background? A major part of the explanation is that how well young people do earlier in the education system has a strong influence on whether they will go to university, and rich and poor students perform markedly differently at school. These large differences in achievement are far from being just of academic concern: they have major implications for policy. In much public and policy discourse about university access, there is an assumption that universities should be doing more to ensure that they enrol a diverse student body. Many commentators have called for universities to do more to help students from poor backgrounds get to university. Indeed, Professor Les Ebdon,

Director of Fair Access to Higher Education, has repeatedly called for universities to make 'further and faster' progress towards reducing the socio-economic gaps in higher education access.[1]

The view that universities must do more is at least partially predicated on the belief that there are high achieving students who should be enrolled in university who are not, and indeed students who should be enrolled in high status universities who are not. However, if in fact the main reason for the low enrolment rate of poor students is their lower achievement in school—as our research suggests is the case—then clearly policy needs to be focused as much on the school system as the point of entry into university. This does not mean that universities have no role to play in increasing the numbers of poor children going to university; rather that this may be best achieved by tackling the low achievement of poor pupils in the school system, rather than encouraging qualified students from poor backgrounds to aspire to or apply to university.

This chapter and the next present the latest empirical evidence on the role of prior achievement in explaining socio-economic differences in university entry for England. This chapter focuses on the importance of secondary school exam results, including how much it matters which subjects young people choose to study. It also compares the findings for England to those from other Anglophone countries. We saw in Chapter 1 that England is not unique in having large socio-economic differences in university participation. Drawing on our own analysis for England, Australia, Canada and the USA, we compare the extent to which socio-economic gaps in university participation across the four countries can be explained by differences in young people's achievement at the end of secondary school, to understand the extent to which the causes of socio-economic gaps in university participation may be common across countries.

How do we Define Socio-Economic Background?

In this chapter and the next we discuss differences in the university participation of young people from different socio-economic backgrounds, referring quite loosely to 'poor' or 'disadvantaged', and 'rich' or 'advantaged' students. There are of course many different ways to

[1] Comment on the Prime Minister's comments on fair access, 31 January 2016. See also OFFA's guidance on the access agreements that universities have to produce in order to charge fees above £6,000 per year.

measure an individual's socio-economic position and previous chapters have already used more than one definition. Economists prefer to use the level of income of an individual's household, while sociologists might prefer to use their parents' social class, and geographers would incorporate some measure of the community in which they are located. In practice, however, we are necessarily constrained by the data that are available.

In the school system in England, administrative data are collected on every child and they are comprehensive in terms of recording children's achievement in national tests and public exams. They are less comprehensive, however, when it comes to measuring pupils' socio-economic background. The data include an indicator of whether children attending state schools in England are or have been eligible for free school meals. The data also include pupils' postcodes, but again only for those attending state schools. We can therefore supplement this indicator of eligibility for free school meals with indicators of the neighbourhood in which pupils reside. Chapter 3 drew on information on past entry rates to university in the individual's local area, while here we incorporate average measures of income, education, housing tenure, and other indicators of deprivation from very local neighbourhoods.

Most of the analyses discussed in this chapter rely on grouping pupils on the basis of an index of deprivation, which we derive from a combination of free school meal eligibility and these various neighbourhood measures of socio-economic status.[2] State school students are divided into fifths on the basis of the index, so when we discuss the top and the bottom of the socio-economic distribution we are comparing the fifth most advantaged households to the fifth most disadvantaged households according to this measure. We use 'poor' or 'socio-economically disadvantaged' interchangeably to describe the bottom group and 'rich' or 'socio-economically advantaged' to describe the top group. In some data sources we have more precise indicators of socio-economic background, including parental income or education, and where these are used instead we indicate this in the text. Private school students are generally not included in our analysis unless otherwise specified.

---

[2] See Chowdry, H., Crawford, C., Dearden, L., Goodman, A., and Vignoles, A. (2013), 'Widening participation in higher education: Analysis using linked administrative data', *Journal of the Royal Statistical Society*, Series A, 176: 431–57 for further discussion of the construction of this index, including how it relates to individual measures of socio-economic background from a survey of secondary school pupils.

How much of the Socio-Economic Gap in University Participation can be Explained by Prior Achievement?

It has long been known that, in the USA, children raised in households where parents have low education levels and low income tend to do relatively poorly in school compared to children from more socio-economically advantaged households. This strong link between household circumstances and educational success is particularly acute at university level, where the socio-economic differences in the likelihood of going to university are stark, as already noted in Chapter 1.[3] This rather depressing observation in fact holds true in most countries. The evidence from the USA has also suggested that the low prior achievement of poor children—their weaker performance in high school—is a crucially important factor in explaining their low university enrolment rate.

That said, US evidence also suggests that there remain large differences in the likelihood of going to university between individuals with higher and lower levels of parental education and indeed higher and lower levels of parental income, even if we take account of their academic achievement in high school. In other words, given similar academic achievement, poorer students and those whose parents have less education are still less likely to enrol in a four-year college (for a Bachelors degree) than their more advantaged counterparts. Some have also argued that the 'conditional gap' measured in terms of parental income—how much less likely a poor student is to go to university than an equivalently qualified rich student—has been increasing over time.[4] This implies that, in the USA at least, there are problems related to access to university that go beyond poor children and those from less educated backgrounds having low levels of academic achievement in school. Such problems might include credit constraints—an inability to access finance to help cover fees and living costs whilst at university of the type we discussed in Chapter 2. Work that spans several countries has also pointed to an important role for young people's aspirations and expectations in influencing their participation in higher education, as well as

---

[3] See also Carneiro, P. and Heckman, J. (2002), 'The evidence on credit constraints in post-secondary schooling', *Economic Journal*, 112(482): 705–34; Cunha, F., Heckman, J., Lochner, L., and Masterov, D. (2006), 'Interpreting the Evidence on Life Cycle Skill Formation', in Hanushek, E. and Welch, F. (eds), *Handbook of the Economics of Education, Volume 1*, Amsterdam: Holland North.

[4] Belley, P. and Lochner, L. (2007), 'The changing role of family income and ability in determining educational achievement', *Journal of Human Capital*, 1(1): 37–89. Duncan, G. and Murnane, R. (2012), *Whither Opportunity: Rising Inequality, Schools, and Children's Life Changes*, New York: Russell Sage Foundation.

the expectations and norms of their family and peers.[5] In our research we wanted to understand whether prior attainment is 'the whole ball-game' in England.

There are of course a number of reasons why we might think the situation in England is different. Although there are now relatively high tuition fees in England too, the financial support provided to students is quite different from that offered in the USA. As Chapter 3 has described, students in England are not required to pay any fees prior to study and are entitled to take out a government-backed loan for the full value of their fees (and a contribution towards their living costs), meaning that constraints on the amount or rate at which students can borrow from commercial banks should not unduly influence their enrolment in university. Moreover, these government-backed loans are 'income-contingent', meaning that students do not have to repay them in the event that they have low income after graduation. This effectively puts some of the risk of low returns from university study onto the state rather than the individual graduate. By contrast, loans for higher education in the US tend to be 'mortgage style' loans, for which a set amount needs to be repaid each month, irrespective of the earnings of the graduate, and student loan default has become a big issue. Moreover, while the financial support on offer amongst elite four-year colleges in the US can be extremely generous, support available from other institutions is more variable, and the long and complicated application process has been found to deter some poor students from applying for financial aid.

The comprehensive English administrative data mentioned in the previous section enable us to understand how much of the socio-economic gap in university access can be explained by prior attainment. Are we any different to the USA? These data allow us to follow cohorts of pupils as they progress through the school system and into university, providing us with the means to measure socio-economic gaps in participation in higher education, similar to those discussed in Chapter 1. The fact that they also contain rich measures of achievement from primary and secondary school allows us to compare students with similar academic achievement in order to determine whether differences in the likelihood of enrolling in higher education remain between similarly qualified students.[6]

---

[5] Jackson, M. (ed.) (2013), *Determined to Succeed? Performance versus Choice in Educational Attainment*, Stanford: Stanford University Press.

[6] Studies which have looked at the determinants of socio-economic gaps in educational achievement in England include Chowdry, H., Crawford, C., Dearden, L., Goodman, A., and

Data on students who took their GCSEs in England in 2008, using the measure of socio-economic status described earlier in the chapter, suggest that 56 per cent of the richest fifth of state school students went on to university at age 18 or 19, compared with just 19 per cent of the poorest fifth of state school students, a gap of around 37 percentage points. This is a very large difference, although—as we saw in Chapter 4—there is some evidence that this gap might have fallen somewhat over the last few years. These differences would be even larger if we included private school students, however, as they are even more likely to go to university than the richest state school students: 74 per cent of students who sat their GCSEs in a private school in 2008 went on to participate in higher education shortly after leaving school.

Figure 5.1 takes as its starting point the gap in the likelihood of going to university between state school students in the top and bottom fifths of the socio-economic distribution. The darker bars show the differences in the chances of attending any university at age 18 or 19; the lighter bars show the differences in the likelihood of attending a high status institution *amongst those who go to university*. The first set of bars illustrates the 'raw differences' we have just described—how much more likely one of the 20 per cent least deprived state school students is to go to university than one of the 20 per cent most deprived state school students, taking into account no other factors.

The other bars show how this gap changes when we allow for differences in attainment at different ages. The middle bars show what happens to the gap in higher education participation rates between the most and least deprived state school students if we allow for differences in achievement in GCSE exams (and equivalent vocational qualifications) taken at age 16 (and no other measurement of achievement, or characteristics other than socio-economic status). They show that there is *no* difference in the likelihood of rich and poor students going to university after accounting for attainment at this age: the socio-economic gap in university participation falls to approximately zero amongst students with similar exam results at the end of compulsory schooling. This means that differences in pupils' achievement at the

Vignoles, A. (2013), 'Widening participation in higher education: Analysis using linked administrative data', *Journal of the Royal Statistical Society*, Series A, 176: 431–57; Anders, J. (2012), 'The link between household income, university applications and university attendance', *Fiscal Studies*, 33(2): 185–210; Ermisch, J. and Del Bono, E. (2012), 'Inequality in Achievements during Adolescence', in Ermisch, J., Jäntti, M., and T. Smeeding (eds), *Inequality from Childhood to Adulthood: A Cross-National Perspective on the Transmission of Advantage*, New York: Russell Sage Foundation.

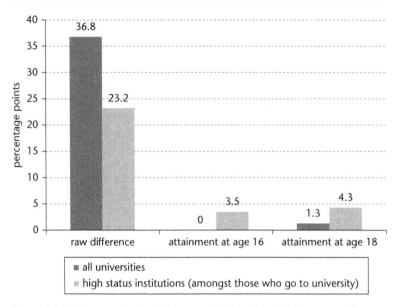

Figure 5.1. Differences in the % of state school students in the top and bottom fifths of the distribution of socio-economic status who go to university, controlling for different measures of attainment

Note: Estimates are for state school students taking their GCSEs in 2008 who go on to university at age 18 or 19. The measure of socio-economic status is as described in the text. Attainment at age 16 refers to performance in exams traditionally taken at the end of secondary schooling (leading to the award of GCSEs and equivalent vocational qualifications). Attainment at age 18 refers to performance in exams traditionally taken two years later, leading to the award of A-levels and equivalent vocational qualifications.

Source: Authors' calculations based on administrative data linking all pupils attending schools in England to all students attending universities in the UK.

end of secondary school can explain virtually *all* of the socio-economic difference in university participation rates that we observe.[7]

Some caution is needed in interpreting this research, since low achievement earlier in the school system is itself likely to have a strong influence on both effort and expectations of students: those who have low expectations about going to university may put in less effort and

---

[7] This leaves little room for discrimination by universities against those from lower socio-economic backgrounds to play a role in explaining the socio-economic differences in participation. Indeed, other research using survey data shows clearly that the socio-economic gap in the rate of entry to higher education is driven by applications to university rather than by decisions universities take on applications (Anders, J. (2012), 'The link between household income, university applications and university attendance', *Fiscal Studies*, 33(2): 185–210).

hence achieve less. Nonetheless it is clear that the gap in achievement that opens up by the time GCSE exams are taken is the key factor in explaining differences in participation in higher education between richer and poorer students.

The last of the darker bars in Figure 5.1 allows for achievement at the end of further education, in A-level exams or their equivalent, usually taken at age 18. It shows that A-level achievement alone actually explains less of the difference in participation rates between richer and poorer students than GCSE results. One potential explanation for this is that students make decisions about university—and universities make decisions about applicants—knowing only their GCSE results and a set of predicted A-level grades, as applications are processed before students receive their final A-level grades. Hence the former may be more predictive of enrolment.

The evidence above would seem to point to the need for action in the school system to raise poor pupils' achievement levels and indeed there has been some progress in this regard, as we discussed in Chapter 4, with a slight narrowing of the achievement gap at GCSE between pupils who are and are not eligible for free school meals.[8] These small reductions in the socio-economic gap in attainment at the end of compulsory schooling may result in a narrowing of the socio-economic gap in university participation as these children pass through the system and potentially enter higher education. Hence there may be some grounds for optimism on this issue in the future. But the achievement gaps (and the gaps in university participation) between those from different socio-economic backgrounds are still very large indeed and are not coming down anywhere near as quickly as we might like.

What about Differences in Institution and Subject Choice?

In the discussion so far we have largely focused on whether or not a student goes to any university. As outlined in Chapter 1, however, there are significant differences in returns to different types of university and indeed to different subjects. It is therefore important not only to consider differences in whether students go to any university, but also the type of university that students attend and the subjects that they choose to study. In particular, it is important to understand whether poorer students with similar levels of achievement are less likely to go to a high

[8] https://www.gov.uk/government/publications/social-mobility-indicators/social-mobility-indicators#attainment-at-age-16-by-free-school-meal-eligibility.

status university or to study a high return subject compared to their richer peers.

The lighter bars in Figure 5.1 present the results for high status institutions. This is the group of around 40 universities that we introduced in Chapter 1 which are ranked highest in terms of research quality, and on which we focus when considering 'high status' institutions throughout the rest of the book.

The first set of bars shows that, amongst state school students who go to university, those from the 20 per cent least deprived backgrounds are about 23 percentage points more likely to attend a high status institution than those from the 20 per cent most deprived backgrounds (38 per cent vs. 15 per cent). This means that just 3 per cent of the 20 per cent poorest state school students attend a high status university at age 18 or 19 (15 per cent of 19 per cent) compared with around a fifth of the 20 per cent richest state school students. (These figures offer a similar picture to that presented in Figure 4.4.) And once again the figures are even higher for those who previously attended a private school at age 16: 60 per cent of private school students who go to university attend a high status institution, meaning that nearly half of those who sat their GCSEs in a private school went on to a high status university at age 18 or 19.

As was the case for participation overall, however, much of this difference in the likelihood of attending a high status institution between state school students from different backgrounds is attributable to the fact that poorer students do less well in school. The second and third bars respectively show that the gap falls to about 3.5 percentage points once we allow for prior achievement in either GCSE exams and their equivalents taken at age 16 or A-level exams and their equivalents taken at age 18. Hence it is again the case that much of the explanation for why poor students are so much less likely to study at high status universities is down to their weaker prior achievement.[9] But, in contrast to participation at any UK university, the gap conditional on GCSE attainment is not quite zero. This suggests that there may be some reasons, over and above how well they do in school, that explain why young people from poorer backgrounds are less likely to apply to top universities (or less likely to get in).

Research using data on university applications and admissions has suggested that individuals from lower social classes—those whose parents

_____

[9] See also Anders, J. (2012), 'The link between household income, university applications and university attendance', *Fiscal Studies*, 33(2): 185–210, who reaches the same conclusion using a different data source.

work in manual or routine non-manual jobs, such as working on an assembly line in a factory or as a receptionist in a hairdressers—and those from state schools are less likely to apply to Russell Group universities than those whose parents work in higher professional or managerial occupations, or those who attend a private school.[10] Conditional on having applied to one of these top institutions, there are also further socio-economic differences in the likelihood of receiving an offer of a place from the university in question. Moreover, these findings hold even comparing applicants with the same A-level attainment. This suggests that some of the remaining unexplained gap in participation at high status institutions between those from more and less deprived families arises because individuals from lower socio-economic backgrounds are less likely to apply to these top institutions and, conditional on applying, less likely to get in.

It is not clear what is driving these lower application and offer rates. Research based on interviews with potential university applicants has suggested that some individuals from lower socio-economic backgrounds feel constrained in terms of the universities to which they apply, either for geographic reasons—wanting or needing to live close to or at home—or for psychological reasons, such as concerns about not fitting in.[11] This suggests that tackling these issues may be an important complement to ensuring that students from lower socio-economic backgrounds have the right grades to get to these top institutions.

Even less is known about why some students appear to be less likely to receive offers from certain institutions than others, though the fact that university offers are made on the basis of predicted A-level grades and recommendations from schools, rather than actual grades achieved, may be relevant if more disadvantaged students have lower grade predictions or weaker recommendations from their schools.[12]

Amongst those who go to university, there are not only differences in terms of the type of institution attended between those from richer and poorer backgrounds, but also differences in the subjects they study. These differences are not systematic, however: for example, while those from higher socio-economic backgrounds are more likely to study high

[10] Boliver, V. (2013), 'How fair is access to more prestigious UK universities?' *The British Journal of Sociology*, 64(2): 344–64.

[11] See, for example, Reay, D., Davies, J., David, M., and Ball, S. (2001), 'Choices of degree or degrees of choice? class, "race" and the higher education choice process', *Sociology*, 35(4): 855–74.

[12] The accuracy of predicted grades has certainly been found to be lower for those from lower socio-economic backgrounds. See, for example, BIS (2013), 'Investigating the accuracy of predicted A-level grades as part of the 2010 UCAS admission process', Department for Business, Innovation and Skills Research Paper 120.

return subjects like medicine, veterinary sciences, maths, engineering and economics, those from lower socio-economic backgrounds are more likely to study high return subjects like biology, computer science, business and law. Differences in school achievement play a clear role in explaining these choices, with the differences generally reduced—and in some cases reversed—once we account for prior attainment. For example, students from lower socio-economic backgrounds are actually more likely to go on to study maths at university than their equivalently qualified peers from higher socio-economic backgrounds.

Does Subject Choice at School Explain the Socio-Economic Gaps in University Entry?

Thus far we have suggested that a substantial part of the explanation for poor children's lower application and enrolment rates in university is their weaker prior achievement. There is, however, an additional element to the story. It is not simply the case that poorer children have lower achievement in school. It is also true that they take different subjects at GCSE and A-level. There are at least two ways in which subject choice earlier in the school system may matter for higher education participation. First, some subjects are required for certain degrees: to study physics at university almost certainly requires three science subjects at A-level. By contrast, to study economics at university does not generally require A-level economics (although it may need A-level maths). Different subject choices at GCSE and A-level may therefore help to explain some of the socio-economic differences in degree subject described above.

Second, some subjects are more desirable for high status universities than others. The Russell Group of universities have started publicizing the importance of a set of subjects—known as 'facilitating subjects'—which are more attractive to them.[13] These include English, maths, sciences, humanities and languages. Subject choice earlier in the school system may therefore be particularly relevant when considering why, even amongst those who go to university, young people from lower socio-economic backgrounds are less likely to receive offers from and enrol in higher status universities.

---

[13] Russell Group (2015), *Informed Choices: A Russell Group Guide to Making Decisions about Post-16 Education*, Russell Group, Fourth Edition.

Table 5.1. A-level students taking 'facilitating' subjects (%), by socio-economic status, 2004–10

	Number of facilitating subjects		
	1 or more %	2 or more %	3 or more %
State school pupils by socio-economic group:			
1st (bottom)	60	32	13
2nd	63	33	14
3rd	65	35	15
4th	68	38	16
5th (top)	72	43	19
Private school pupils	82	56	28

Notes: the table is restricted to those students passing at least two A-levels at grades A–E in any subject between 2004 and 2010. The number of 'facilitating' subjects also refers to passes at grades A–E; see the text for the definition of these subjects.

Source: authors' calculations based on administrative data linking all pupils attending schools in England to all students attending universities in the UK.

One way we can look at the potential importance of subject choice is to consider the proportions of students taking qualifications in the 'facilitating' subjects preferred by the Russell Group. Table 5.1 shows the percentage of students taking different numbers of 'facilitating' A-levels between 2004 and 2010, amongst a group of students who achieved passes in at least two A-levels in any subject. The differences between richer and poorer students are striking. For example, while just under a third of the poorest group of students take two or more facilitating subjects, more than half of all private school students do so.

These differences may of course be partially driven by differences in prior attainment at GCSE between more and less advantaged students. Table 5.2 shows, by socio-economic background, what proportion of students who achieved at least five A*–C grades at GCSE between 2002 and 2008 obtained high numbers of these grades in facilitating subjects. (These subjects are the same as those that comprise the 'English baccalaureate', a new standard of achievement introduced by the Conservative–Liberal Democrat coalition government that came to power in 2010.) For example, only around 17 per cent of the poorest students achieved six or more A*–C grades in English baccalaureate subjects, whilst 70 per cent of private school students did so.

However, even amongst students who study similar subjects and achieve similarly high grades at the end of secondary school, there are still differences in A-level and university subject choice. For example, amongst those who achieve six or more A*–C grades in facilitating

Table 5.2. GCSE students taking English baccalaureate ('EBacc') subjects (%), by socio-economic status, 2002–8

	Number of 'EBacc' subjects taken			
	4 or more %	5 or more %	6 or more %	Total Av.
State school pupils by socio-economic group:				
1st (bottom)	60	38	17	4
2nd	69	49	25	4
3rd	76	58	33	5
4th	81	65	41	5
5th (top)	87	74	52	5
Private school pupils	94	85	70	6

Notes: The table is restricted to pupils who sat GCSEs between 2002 and 2008 and achieved five or more passes at grades A*–C. The number of 'EBacc' subjects also refers to passes at grades A*–C; see the text for the definition of these subjects. The final column gives the average number of EBacc subjects taken, rounded to the nearest whole number.

Source: Authors' calculations based on administrative data linking all pupils attending schools in England to all students attending universities in the UK.

subjects at GCSE level, around half of the richest state school students and nearly two thirds of private school students go on to acquire at least one A-level in a facilitating subject, while less than a third of the poorest state school students do the same.

Figure 5.2 provides further insight into the implications of rich and poor students making different subject choices at GCSE and A-level in terms of university participation. The figures show the socio-economic gap in participation before and after allowing for subject choice at GCSE and A-level. The lighter shaded bars show the socio-economic gap when just allowing for GCSE or A-level achievement. The darker bars show the gap when also allowing for *subject choice* at GCSE and A-level. In both cases the socio-economic gap is reduced when we allow for subject choice, but only when considering participation at higher status institutions (the right hand set of bars). This reflects what we have just shown: that, on average, poor students take different subjects at GCSE and A-level to those taken by richer students, but that this difference matters most when applying to higher status institutions who perhaps give greater weight to whether students hold the required grades in the set of facilitating subjects described earlier. But while there is an additional small narrowing of the socio-economic gap when we allow for subject choice, it does not make a great deal of difference. This suggests that differences in subject availability and choice are not responsible for a major part of the socio-economic gap in university entry.

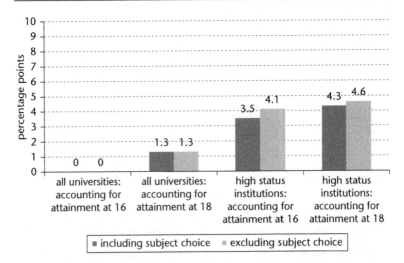

Figure 5.2. Differences in the % of state school students in the top and bottom fifths of the distribution of socio-economic status who go to university, controlling for different measures of attainment (including and excluding subject choice)

Note: Estimates are for state-school students taking their GCSEs in 2008 who go on to university at age 18 or 19. The measure of socio-economic status is as described in the text. Attainment at age 16 refers to performance in exams traditionally taken at the end of secondary schooling (leading to the award of GCSEs and equivalent vocational qualifications). Attainment at age 18 refers to performance in exams traditionally taken two years later, leading to the award of A-levels and equivalent vocational qualifications. The dark bars show results controlling for the subjects studied at ages 16 and 18 as well as the qualifications and grades attained. The light bars show results without accounting for the subjects studied.

Source: Authors' calculations based on administrative data linking all pupils attending schools in England to all students attending universities in the UK.

In summary, the most up-to-date evidence we have for England suggests that weaker achievement plays a substantial role in explaining why poorer students are less likely to end up at university at all and less likely to enrol in a high status institution studying a high return subject. Subject choice at GCSE and A-level plays a smaller role, but only for attendance at high status institutions. Comparing these findings with the evidence on the drivers of socio-economic differences in college attendance amongst US students presented earlier in this section suggests that prior attainment may be a more important explanatory factor for students in England than for students in the USA. However, these studies draw on completely different types of data and analysis. Does the same picture emerge with comparable data?

What can International Evidence Tell Us?

As we noted at the start of the chapter, we can draw on quite similar data from Australia, Canada, England and the USA to compare the relationship between family background and pupil achievement in secondary school across these countries, and the implications of these differences for students' likelihood of going to university to study for a Bachelor's degree.[14] We have selected these countries partly due to the similarities between their education systems and partly because, as in the UK, higher education is an important route to labour market success.

Unsurprisingly, and in line with the evidence we described in Chapter 1, we find that—just as in England—there are large differences in the likelihood of going to university between young people from different social backgrounds in these countries. The data we use have good measures of family background, including detailed information on parental income and parental education level. We focus particularly on differences between young people who have highly educated (graduate) parents and those whose parents have low levels of qualifications, i.e. below high school (age 18).

In England, students who have a graduate parent are around 49 percentage points more likely to go to university than students who have parents with low qualifications. This gap is similar in the USA and Canada, but smaller in Australia, at around 34 percentage points.[15] Differences in prior achievement between advantaged and disadvantaged pupils play a major role in explaining differences in university entry in all these countries, however. Once we allow for differences in pupil achievement, in all four countries the socio-economic gap in participation in higher education is dramatically reduced. This is an

---

[14] This excludes two-year associate degrees in the USA. Although some two-year college students may eventually complete a four-year degree, as noted in Chapter 1, upgrade rates remain low. Exclusion of these students means we may be slightly understating the participation rate in higher education of poorer students in the USA as this group is the most likely to enrol for a two-year degree. Our findings in this section are drawn from Jerrim, J., Vignoles, A., and Finnie, R. (2012), 'University access for disadvantaged children: A comparison across English speaking countries', Department of Quantitative Social Science Working Paper 12-11, Institute of Education, University of London.

[15] The finding of a similar family background gap in the USA compared to England appears to contrast with the evidence in Chapter 1. However, the international comparison in Figure 1.8 focuses on the likelihood of going to university for students who have low educated parents (below high school graduation). Here in Chapter 5 we focus on the likelihood of going to university for students with graduate parents. OECD (2012), *Education at a Glance*, Paris: OECD, Table A6.2 suggests that students with graduate parents have similar odds of attending university in the UK and USA, although the OECD comparison is skewed by the exclusion from the US data of lower level 'associate degrees', which also affects our Figure 1.8, as we noted in Chapter 1.

important finding. It implies that the endemic underachievement of disadvantaged students in the school system is the main reason why those from poor backgrounds are so much less likely to go to university than their richer peers across all four countries.

That said, poor prior achievement seems to play a more important role in explaining why poor children in England are less likely to go to university than in Canada, Australia or the USA. In these three countries it seems that there is a weaker link between prior achievement and university enrolment. For example, in England about 80 per cent of the socio-economic gap in the likelihood of going to university can be explained by differences in prior achievement. By contrast, only 60 per cent of the gap is explained by prior achievement in the USA, 55 per cent in Australia and 30 per cent in Canada.[16]

The findings imply that in England there is a closer link between prior achievement and university admission. In other countries, the large socio-economic gaps in higher education participation must be explained by other factors. Such factors may include the credit constraints faced by poorer students and differences in aspirations and expectations for higher education across different socio-economic groups. There is certainly a sizeable literature which provides support for both of these explanations in countries such as the USA. In England, however, it is clear that universities are more academically selective and students are admitted more on the basis of their prior achievement than on the basis of other factors, such as their social background. One might argue this is meritocratic. Equally, however, it is also true that the socio-economic gap in prior achievement is very large in England, so even if universities selected students only on the basis of those measures, this will have the effect of ensuring that in overall terms social background matters more for university admission in England.

In this work we were also able to consider the type of university attended by students in each country. Hence we could determine the

---

[16] There remains a difference in the likelihood of going to university between those from more and less advantaged backgrounds in England using these data. There are a number of reasons why the percentage of the raw gap in higher education participation explained here is somewhat less than that reported using administrative data earlier in the chapter: the data are from a slightly different cohort, use a different measure of socio-economic background and, perhaps most importantly, account for a much wider set of characteristics. This may have the effect of widening socio-economic gaps if we control for factors that are positively associated with going to university, but are more common amongst those from lower socio-economic backgrounds. Ethnicity is a good example of such a characteristic: ethnic minorities are over-represented amongst the most disadvantaged pupils, but are also substantially more likely to go to university than White British students (see, for example, Crawford, C. and Greaves, E. (2015), *Socio-economic, ethnic and gender differences in HE participation*, Report to the Department for Business, Innovation and Skills).

importance of prior achievement in explaining attendance at higher status universities as well. We found that differences in prior achievement were equally important across all four countries, but did not entirely explain why poor students are so much less likely to enrol in a more elite university. In other words, if we compare two students with similar levels of achievement, the student with more highly educated parents is more likely to enrol in a high status university, regardless of the country of interest. Hence England is not unique in this regard and these results imply that one focus of policy across all these nations should be to ensure that very well qualified poor students are encouraged to apply to the highest status university that they can achieve.

Summing Up

The findings discussed in this chapter highlight the crucial importance of prior attainment for university entry, and hence its importance in explaining the large socio-economic gaps in higher education participation that we observe in England. How well students perform at the end of compulsory schooling—in terms of their grades in GCSEs and equivalent qualifications—plays a particularly key role in understanding why poorer students are less likely to end up at university than their richer peers, even more so than A-level qualifications, which may reflect the fact that GCSE grades are often the only realized measures of attainment available to universities when making entry decisions. Prior attainment is also an important part of the reason why poorer students are less likely to attend high status institutions, with subject choice apparently a more important factor at these institutions than at other universities. Ensuring that students from poor backgrounds get good grades in facilitating subjects at GCSE and A-levels may therefore contribute to increasing their chances of making it to a high status institution, although overall attainment (in terms of qualifications and grades) remains the most important determinant of these outcomes.

Comparing three countries that have many similar features to the English education system suggests that the role of prior achievement in explaining why those from higher socio-economic backgrounds are so much more likely to go to university than their peers from lower socio-economic backgrounds is somewhat stronger in England than in Australia, Canada or the USA. These findings represent a challenge for English policymakers: it may be that England's system of higher education with its 'rigorous' entry standards, i.e. high levels of required prior achievement, disadvantages poor students to a greater degree than systems in countries where academic standards are less strictly required, although it is also possible that there are other explanations for the patterns we observe.

Given the vital importance of socio-economic differences in attainment at the end of secondary school for explaining socio-economic differences in university access, it seems important to understand when exactly these differences in achievement emerge and what governments, schools and universities may be able to do to help overcome them. We turn to this issue in Chapter 6.

6

When and How to Intervene to Increase University Attendance?

Chapter 5 showed that attainment at age 16 plays a crucial role in explaining socio-economic differences in participation in higher education, including at high status institutions. But we also know that differences in achievement between children from different social backgrounds emerge as early as pre-school. This leaves open the question of when best to intervene to increase young people's attainment at the end of secondary schooling in order to influence their chances of continuing on to higher education. Evidence from James Heckman, Nobel prize-winning economist, and his co-authors stresses the notion that 'skills beget skills'. This suggests that intervening early may be the best way to increase attainment at the end of compulsory schooling. But we also know that early interventions by themselves are not enough: children from poor backgrounds who benefit from additional support in their pre-school years have still been found to fall behind their peers from wealthier backgrounds when those 'early investments' are not followed up during their school careers.[1]

In this chapter, we document the differences in earlier school achievement between young people from different socio-economic backgrounds and show just how important these differences are in explaining subsequent gaps in higher education participation. This should illustrate when socio-economic gaps in achievement emerge, and hence provide insight into the potentially critical periods for intervention to raise

[1] See, for example, Currie, J. and Thomas, D. (2000), 'School quality and the longer-term effects of Head Start', *Journal of Human Resources*, 35: 755–74; Cunha, F. and Heckman, J. (2007), 'The Technology of Skill Formation', *The American Economic Review*, 97: 31–47; Cunha, F., Heckman, J., Lochner, L., and Masterov, D. (2006), 'Interpreting the Evidence on Life Cycle Skill Formation', in Hanushek, E. and Welch, F. (eds), *Handbook of the Economics of Education, Volume 1*, Amsterdam: Holland North.

university attendance. We also consider some of the mechanisms through which these large differences in achievement might arise. Specifically, we consider differences in the schools attended by more and less socio-economically advantaged students, and in their expectations about whether or not they will go to university. Of course, we do not attempt to consider *all* the factors that explain why poor children do relatively badly in school, which would require a different book.

When do Socio-Economic Gaps in Achievement Emerge?

Chapter 5 focused on the extent to which the large differences in university attendance by socio-economic background can be explained by differences in achievement at 16 and 18, finding that exam results at these ages appear to play a vital role in explaining the socio-economic gaps in university attendance in England, indeed a more important role than in the three other countries considered. However, understanding in more detail *when* these socio-economic gaps in achievement emerge is also critical if we are to pinpoint when interventions are needed. If socio-economic differences in achievement are evident by the time pupils start school, and stay relatively constant as children move through the school system, then clearly intervention is needed early in a pupil's life. If, on the other hand, differences in school achievement widen as children progress through the education system, particularly during certain periods, then interventions in primary or secondary schooling may be especially productive. Of course, to resolve these debates we need good current evidence on the extent to which the differences in university enrolment can be explained by measures of prior achievement taken at different ages.

Figure 6.1 adds to Figure 5.1 from Chapter 5, illustrating how much of the difference in university attendance between the 20 per cent most and least deprived state school students can be accounted for using earlier measures of pupils' achievement, at ages 7 and 11. The dark bars again focus on participation at any UK university, while the lighter bars focus on participation at the group of 41 high status institutions introduced in Chapter 1. The first set of bars illustrates the raw differences in participation. Compared to these raw differences, allowing for achievement at age 7 (in the second set of bars) reduces the unexplained difference in participation at any UK university between pupils from the richest and poorest families by around 10 percentage points, from around 37 to around 27 percentage points. The gap is reduced further, to around 20 percentage points, if we instead allow for differences in

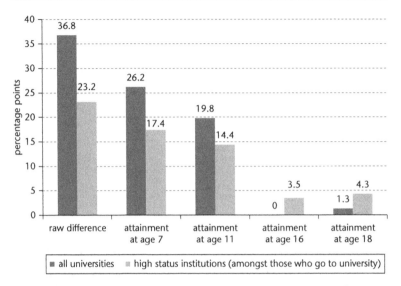

Figure 6.1. Differences in the % of state school students in the top and bottom fifths of the distribution of socio-economic status who go to university, controlling for different measures of attainment

Note: estimates are for state school students taking their GCSEs in 2008 who go on to university at age 18 or 19. The measure of socio-economic status is as described in the text. Attainment at age 16 refers to performance in exams traditionally taken at the end of secondary schooling (leading to the award of GCSEs and equivalent vocational qualifications). Attainment at age 18 refers to performance in exams traditionally taken two years later, leading to the award of A-levels and equivalent vocational qualifications.

Source: authors' calculations based on administrative data linking all pupils attending schools in England to all students attending universities in the UK.

students' achievement at age 11—and, as we saw in Chapter 5, it falls even further if we account for attainment at age 16 or 18. We see a similar picture in terms of the socio-economic differences in participation at high status institutions amongst those who go to university (the lighter bars).

The fact that we are able to explain more and more of the socio-economic gap in university participation rates by controlling for later and later measures of achievement suggests that socio-economic differences in children's achievement emerge early and widen over time. Work by some of us for the Social Mobility and Child Poverty Commission has documented the socio-economic gaps that are observed as children move through the English school system.[2] This

---

[2] Crawford, C., Macmillan, L., and Vignoles, A. (2014), *Progress Made by High-Attaining Children from Disadvantaged Backgrounds*, Social Mobility and Child Poverty Commission

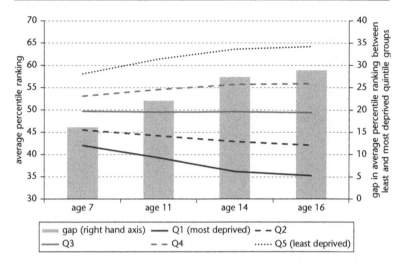

Figure 6.2. Average academic achievement (percentile rank) amongst state school students by age and socio-economic background, and the gap between the most and least deprived quintile groups

Note: achievement is measured using percentile rankings based on average reading and maths scores in national achievement tests at age 7, and average English and maths scores in national achievement tests at ages 11, 14, and 16. Analysis is conducted on children who were born between September 1990 and August 1991, who attended a non-special state secondary school and for whom we observe English and maths test scores at each age.

Source: Crawford, C., Macmillan, L., and Vignoles, A. (2015), 'When and why do initially high attaining poor children fall behind?' Social Policy in a Cold Climate Working Paper 20, Centre for Analysis of Social Exclusion, London School of Economics.

research focuses on a cohort of children born in 1990/91 and follows them throughout compulsory schooling using the same administrative data and the same measure of socio-economic background described in Chapter 5.

Figure 6.2 uses these data to show the trajectories of students from different socio-economic backgrounds as they progress through the education system. State school pupils are divided into fifths on the basis of our index of socio-economic status. The average percentile rank of the children's achievement within each fifth of the distribution of socio-economic status is plotted at ages 7, 11, 14 and 16, with 1 being

Research Report, June 2014. This research was updated and extended in Crawford, C., Macmillan, L., and Vignoles, A. (2015), 'When and why do initially high attaining poor children fall behind?' Social Policy in a Cold Climate Working Paper 20, Centre for Analysis of Social Exclusion, London School of Economics.

the rank of the lowest scoring child and 100 being the rank of the highest scoring child in national achievement tests at these ages.

The picture is striking. Even at age 7 we observe substantial differences in average school achievement by family background. If there were no differences in achievement by socio-economic background, we would expect the average percentile rank of each of the five groups to be around 50. By age 7, however, children from the richest fifth of families have average achievement levels at around the 58th percentile, while children from the poorest fifth of families have average achievement levels at around the 42nd percentile. The socio-economic gap on this measure is therefore around 16 places in a ranking from 1 to 100. Moreover, the difference in rankings increases as children get older. By the end of primary school (at age 11), it has risen to around 22 ranking places and by the end of secondary school (age 16) to around 29 ranking places.

Whilst documenting and understanding average socio-economic gaps in pupil achievement and how they change through the school system is important, it is also important to understand the educational progress made by children who, at age 7, scored similarly in national achievement tests. We therefore compared the trajectories of children who, at age 7, showed similar academic 'potential', but who came from different socio-economic backgrounds. We were particularly interested in understanding how initially high achieving poor children fare in the English education system compared to initially high achieving children from richer backgrounds, since these higher achieving children are the ones that are most likely to go to university and in particular most likely to go to a higher status university.

Figure 6.3 shows the trajectories of high, average, and low achieving pupils, as defined by their scores in the nationally set maths test taken by all pupils in state schools in England at age 7.[3] The trajectories are shown just for children in the top and bottom fifths of the distribution of socio-economic status.[4] As in Figure 6.2, we plot the average percentile rank of the children's test scores at each age. It is evident from the graph that, by the end of compulsory schooling, there is a wide

[3] High achievement is defined as scoring above expectation (Level 3) in maths at Key Stage 1, average achievement as scoring at the expected level (Level 2) and low achievement as scoring below expectation (Level 1).

[4] When doing these kinds of analyses there can be a problem with the phenomenon known as 'regression to the mean'. This is when initially high achieving pupils appear to fall behind, but that this is either because their earlier result was just due to luck or because of mismeasurement of their achievement. We address this problem in a number of ways in Crawford et al. (2014), *Progress Made by High-Attaining Children from Disadvantaged Backgrounds.*

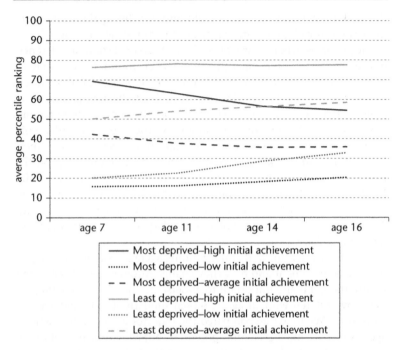

Figure 6.3. Average academic achievement (percentile rank) amongst state school students from age 7 to age 16, by initial achievement and socio-economic background

Note: initial achievement grouping is defined using maths scores taken at age 7. Achievement is measured using percentile rankings based on reading scores in national achievement tests at age 7 and English scores in national achievement tests at ages 11, 14, and 16. Analysis is conducted on children who were born between September 1990 and August 1991, who attended a non-special state secondary school and for whom we observe English and maths test scores at each age.

Source: Crawford, C., Macmillan, L., and Vignoles, A. (2015), 'When and why do initially high attaining poor children fall behind?' Social Policy in a Cold Climate Working Paper 20, Centre for Analysis of Social Exclusion, London School of Economics.

socio-economic gap in achievement between children who were initially classed as high achieving. At the end of primary school (age 11), children in the least deprived fifth (the top fifth) of the socio-economic distribution with high initial achievement score on average at the 78th percentile, while the poorest fifth of children who were initially classed as high achieving are only recorded as scoring at the 63rd percentile on average. This 15-point gap widens further as children progress through the education system so that by the end of compulsory schooling (at age 16) this group of initially high achieving poor children have fallen behind their richer but initially lower attaining counterparts. A similar picture emerges if we were to instead compare children who were initially average attaining or initially low attaining: socio-economic gaps in achievement emerge between children who scored similarly at age 7.

The patterns emerging from this research are concerning. Students from poor backgrounds who are high scoring at age 7 seem to be much less likely to maintain this high achievement trajectory than their richer peers. This fall away in the relative achievement of children from poor backgrounds appears to occur largely in early secondary school, between age 11 and age 14. These results highlight the importance of secondary school as a potentially crucial time for intervention to sustain the achievement of initially high achieving pupils from poor backgrounds. If the early promise shown by these children can be sustained, then it is far more likely that they will go on to university and indeed that they will attend a high status university. Indeed, the relatively limited robust quantitative evidence on interventions designed specifically to increase the university participation rates of those from lower socio-economic backgrounds suggest that the most effective interventions start early and are sustained.[5]

What Role do Secondary Schools Play in Explaining Socio-Economic Differences in Pupils' Achievement?

The previous section demonstrated clearly that socio-economic gaps in achievement emerge early, but also that they widen as children move through the school system, particularly during secondary school. Given the importance of attainment at the end of secondary school in explaining the large socio-economic differences in university access that are the focus of this book, this suggests that understanding the drivers of attainment at age 16 is at the heart of understanding when and how best to intervene to increase the participation rates of poorer students in higher education. So what does drive the very large differences in pupil achievement at the end of secondary school? There are many factors that influence pupil achievement, ranging from those related to the individual student, their family, their teachers, their school and their communities. It would be the subject of an entirely different book

[5] See, for example, Moore, J., Sanders, J., and Higham, L. (2013), *Literature review of research into widening participation to higher education*, Report to Hefce and OFFA by Aimhigher Research and Consultancy Network.

to try to explain the very many ways that pupils' socio-economic status influences their education achievement.[6] As we have shown secondary school to be a potentially critical period for intervention, however, we focus on the role of secondary schools in explaining socio-economic differences in pupil achievement, as they are one obvious vehicle through which policymakers can intervene to try to improve the achievement of children from poorer backgrounds.

The first point to note is that children from different socio-economic backgrounds tend to go to different schools. This arises most obviously in the case of private schools, attended by around 7 per cent of pupils in England at age 16, where average day fees of around £4,500 per term are likely to preclude all but the wealthiest families from attending.[7] Indeed, survey data suggests that private school students come from families which are estimated to have more than double the median income of families of students who attend state schools.[8] But it also arises because most state schools admit students at least partly on the basis of proximity—the nearer to the school a family lives, the more likely their children are to be admitted—meaning that richer families can purchase houses near to sought-after state-funded schools.[9] And there are also still a small number of schools which admit students on the basis of academic achievement, in which pupils from richer families are over-represented. These 'selective' state schools (or grammar schools) serve an even smaller percentage of the population than private schools in England (just 3.5 per cent), but they, on average, have much higher attainment than those attending private schools when they arrive.

If all children had the same chance of attending a school of similar quality, then we would expect to see roughly the same percentage of pupils in each school being eligible for free school meals, at around the

[6] Two books that address this issue are Duncan, G. and Murnane, R. (2011), *Whither Opportunity: Rising Inequality, Schools, and Children's Life Changes*, New York: Russell Sage Foundation; and Ermisch, J., Jäntti, M., and Smeeding, T. (eds) (2012), *From Parents to Children: The Intergenerational Transmission of Advantage*, New York: Russell Sage Foundation.

[7] *Source*: Independent Schools Council Census 2015.

[8] The median refers to someone in the middle of the distribution, with income above 50% of the relevant population and below 50% of the relevant population. The median is often used in preference to average (or mean) income because averages can be biased by small numbers of individuals with very high incomes. The figures for family income, which are adjusted for differences in family size, are based on the Longitudinal Study of Young People in England, and taken from Anders, J. (2014), 'Does an aptitude test affect socioeconomic and gender gaps in attendance at an elite university?' Department of Quantitative Social Science Working Paper No. 14-07, UCL Institute of Education.

[9] Gibbons, S. and Machin, S. (2003), 'Valuing English primary schools', *Journal of Urban Economics*, 53(2): 197–219; Allen, R., Burgess, S., and Key, T. (2010), 'Choosing secondary school by moving house: School quality and the formation of neighbourhoods', The Centre for Market and Public Organisation Working Paper No. 10/238, University of Bristol.

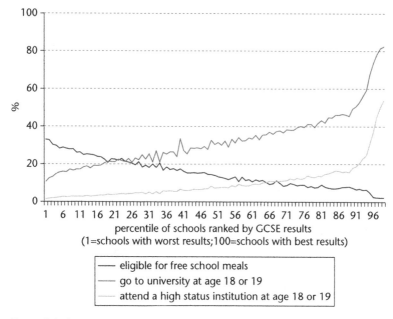

percentile of schools ranked by GCSE results
(1=schools with worst results;100=schools with best results)

— eligible for free school meals
— go to university at age 18 or 19
⋯ attend a high status institution at age 18 or 19

Figure 6.4. Average outcomes amongst pupils at state schools ranked according to the percentage of pupils who achieved 5 A*–C grades in their GCSEs

Notes: estimates are for state schools only (excluding special schools). Schools are ranked according to the average percentage of pupils achieving 5 A*–C grades at GCSE between 2002 and 2008. Average eligibility for free school meals is measured across all pupils in the school over the same period. Pupils are classified according to the school they attended at age 16. The percentage of pupils who go on to university (and to a high status institution) is the average per school estimated across all pupils who sat their GCSEs between 2002 and 2008.

Source: authors' calculations based on administrative data linking all pupils attending schools in England to all students attending universities in the UK.

national average of 14 per cent at age 16 (as of 2015).[10] In fact we see some schools with much higher proportions of pupils eligible for free school meals and some schools with much lower proportions. And there is a strong negative relationship between average school performance and the proportion of pupils in the school who are eligible for free school meals.

Figure 6.4 illustrates this relationship. It splits state secondary schools in England into 100 equally sized groups (percentiles) on the basis of the percentage of pupils in the school who achieve the benchmark of five

[10] See Table 3a in the national tables accompanying Statistical First Release 16/2015 from the Department for Education: 'Schools, pupils and their characteristics—January 2015'.

A*–C grades at GCSE. The lowest performing schools are on the left hand side of the graph and the highest performing schools on the right hand side. The dark grey line plots the average percentage of pupils in schools in each percentile group who are eligible for free school meals. It shows a strong negative relationship between secondary school performance and free school meal eligibility, with around one third of pupils in the lowest performing schools eligible for free school meals, compared to just 2 per cent of pupils in the highest performing schools. In other words, poorer pupils tend to go to lower performing schools.

This matters because of the crucial role achievement at the end of secondary school plays in explaining which pupils go to university: if poorer pupils are likely to go to lower-performing schools, then they are more likely to leave with low qualifications themselves, and hence are less likely to go to university. Certainly, rates of participation in higher education vary considerably by school. For example, pupils attending selective state schools are more than 40 percentage points more likely to go to university and more than 30 percentage points more likely to go to a high status institution than pupils attending non-selective state schools.[11]

This point is further illustrated by Figure 6.4, which additionally plots the percentage of pupils that go to university, including to high status institutions, on the basis of the average performance of their secondary school. Here we see a strongly positive relationship between school performance and university participation, with around one in ten pupils attending the lowest performing secondary schools going to university, on average, compared to more than eight in ten pupils at the highest performing schools. Similarly, there are schools where virtually no students attend a high status university and schools where more than half the cohort does so. University participation rates at the highest-performing 10 per cent of schools—which include many private and grammar schools, and hence are disproportionately attended by pupils from the highest socio-economic backgrounds—are especially high.

How do schools influence their pupils' chances of going to university? The obvious answer is the one alluded to above: that good schools help their pupils to achieve good exam results, which in turn enables them to go to university. In fact, our research suggests that that is the main route through which schools influence university entry rates: once we compare pupils with the same exam results, there are only very small differences

---

[11] Crawford, C. (2014), *The Link between Secondary School Characteristics and HE Participation and Outcomes*, Centre for the Analysis of Youth Transitions Research Report for the Department for Education.

between schools in how likely pupils are to go on to university (or to attend high status institutions).[12] This leaves relatively little room for other factors—such as helping students with university applications or with interview preparation—to play a large role in explaining why pupils from some schools are far more likely to go to university than pupils at other schools, at least at the moment.

The fact that there is such a strong relationship between socio-economic background and school performance might indicate that reforms that aimed to increase the quality of *all* schools in the system, or that tried to change the school admissions process to enable poorer children to access higher quality schools would help reduce the socio-economic difference in university attendance. That has certainly been the aim of some reforms to the school system in England over the last fifty years. For example, one of the first major reforms specifically aimed at reducing socio-economic inequalities in academic achievement was the move to 'comprehensive' schooling in the late 1960s and 1970s. The post-war secondary school system had involved selection on academic ability into 'grammar' schools on the basis of a test at age 11, the '11-plus' exam. Children failing this exam went mainly to 'secondary modern' schools. Grammar schools and private schools largely monopolized the supply of students to universities. Secondary modern schools focused more on vocational education with little expectation of pupils staying on in full-time education past the minimum school leaving age and even less expectation of them going to university.

A popular view is that the grammar schools promoted the chances of working class children, providing an academic route leading to university for the bright child from a humble background. There are undoubtedly many individual examples of this happening. But, overall, the verdict of the bulk of research into the issue is that there was a very strong social gradient in those taking the 11-plus exam and indeed passing it. Children from less advantaged backgrounds were far less likely to succeed in getting into grammar schools and consequently were also far less likely to enter higher education.[13] In most of England and Wales, the dual system of grammar schools and secondary modern schools was phased out and replaced with comprehensive schools admitting all children regardless of ability level. This does appear to

---

[12] Ibid.

[13] See, for example, Archer, L., Hutchings, M., and Ross, A. (2005), *Higher Education and Social Class: Issues of Exclusion and Inclusion*, Abingdon: Routledge. The view that England's remaining grammar schools hold back social mobility has been expressed more recently by Her Majesty's Chief Inspector of Schools, Sir Michael Wilshaw (http://www.theguardian. com/education/2013/dec/14/michael-wilshaw-ofsted-teachers-schools).

have improved the achievement of poorer children at age 16 but did not transform their chances of staying on in school past 16 and going on into higher education.

There have also been other reforms to the school system over the last 20 years that might have been expected to raise standards and perhaps also reduce the gap in achievement between students from different socio-economic backgrounds. For example, since the late 1980s, policymakers have tried to promote parental choice and increase competition between schools in England, the idea being that forcing schools to compete for pupils should be a 'tide that lifts all boats'. More recently still, the government's 'academies' programme has tried to raise attainment by offering schools greater autonomy, including greater freedom over how to spend their budget, with the motivation that headteachers will have greater knowledge of how best to allocate resources in order to benefit pupils in their school. There is some evidence that these reforms (and similar reforms in other countries, notably Sweden and the USA) have led to improvements in educational attainment, although the effects seem to vary a lot for different schools. In England, the offer of greater autonomy has also often gone hand in hand with small increases in school funding, which may also have had beneficial effects for pupils' achievement.[14]

Other reforms have attempted to increase the attainment of poorer pupils more explicitly. For example, the government has, for many years, given schools in disadvantaged areas and those catering for high numbers of disadvantaged pupils higher budgets. This has been made more explicit in recent years with the introduction of the 'pupil premium': extra money—equivalent to an increase in per pupil funding of around 15 per cent in secondary schools in 2015—awarded to schools for every pupil they teach who has been eligible for free school meals in the past six years. It is too early to tell how productively these additional resources have been used, and hence the extent to which they have reduced socio-economic inequalities between or even within schools, but the intention of doing so—and the use of resources as a way of

---

[14] For evidence on the effects of greater autonomy in England, see Clark, D. (2009), 'The performance and competitive effects of school autonomy', *Journal of Political Economy*, 117: 745–83; Eyles, A. and Machin, S. (2015) 'The introduction of academy schools to England's education', Centre for Economic Performance Discussion Paper 1368, London School of Economics. For a summary of the research on charter schools—the equivalent of academies in the USA—see Epple, D., Romano, R., and Zimmer, R. (2015), 'Charter schools: a survey of research on their characteristics and effectiveness', National Bureau for Economic Research Working Paper 21256, Cambridge, Massachusetts.

trying to achieve it—has been a key plank of education policy in England for a number of years.

Is it All About Schools?

Which school a child attends clearly matters for their exam results and hence for how likely they are to go to university, and the previous section pointed to a number of policies that have tried to increase school achievement across all schools. But it is also clear that there is a sizeable gap in higher education participation rates between richer and poorer students amongst pupils *who attend the same schools*. For example, while the difference in university entry rates at age 18/19 between the richest and poorest 20 per cent of state school students, regardless of which school they attend, is around 37 percentage points for the cohort who took their GCSEs in 2008, the gap is still around 30 percentage points when we focus on pupils attending the same schools, and around 27 percentage points amongst pupils attending the same high perform-ing schools. The fact that pupils from poorer backgrounds attend worse-quality schools than pupils from richer backgrounds also only provides part of the reason why initially high achieving poor pupils are more likely to fall behind their better-off peers as they move through the school system (as we showed in Figure 6.3): they still appear to fall behind their better-off classmates, but to a slightly lesser extent.[15]

This suggests that the secondary school a pupil attends may not be the primary reason why poor children are likely to have lower achievement than rich children, and indeed why they are less likely to go to univer-sity. While schools undoubtedly play a vital role, children from poorer backgrounds may not just be attending lower quality schools, on aver-age, than their richer peers, but may also be less likely to receive other investments which might help to produce strong school achievement, such as additional tutoring or extra-curricular activities, or help with their homework. While it is possible that schools might be differentially effective for different pupils, the size of the gap in achievement between pupils from different socio-economic backgrounds that is evident when comparing pupils who attend the same secondary school suggests that these other aspects of a child's experiences outside school are at least as important in explaining the differences in achievement and hence in

---

[15] Crawford, C., Macmillan, L., and Vignoles, A. (2015), 'When and why do initially high attaining poor children fall behind?' Social Policy in a Cold Climate Working Paper 20, Centre for Analysis of Social Exclusion, London School of Economics.

university participation as school factors, and of course these non-school factors may be harder to influence via policy.[16]

What types of factors might be important in explaining these socio-economic differences in achievement and hence in university participation that exist even within schools? Again we do not attempt to provide an exhaustive review of these topics, as this would require another book, but instead highlight some examples of the types of factors that might matter. One potentially important factor is pupils' expectations. In public discourse there is often an assumption that poorer students have low expectations about their likelihood of going to university and that this partly explains their low progression rates and also their weak academic achievement.

Our research confirms that poor students are less likely to believe that they are going to go to university than students from the richest families.[17] Figure 6.5 shows the percentage of teenagers in England who believe they are 'very likely' or 'fairly likely' to apply to higher education and how this figure changes from age 14 to age 17. These figures are based on a survey of teenagers who were age 13/14 in 2003/4 and were followed over time, being asked the same question each year about their expectations. (The survey covers teenagers at both state and private schools.) The information that was collected from their parents included household income, and the teenagers are classified into five equal-sized groups on this basis, from the richest fifth to the poorest fifth (averaging income for each household over the four-year period when the child was aged 14–17).

Figure 6.5 shows that there is a 30 percentage point gap in the likelihood of a 14-year-old from the poorest fifth believing they are very or fairly likely to apply to university as compared to a child from the top fifth. Yet, despite this large socio-economic gap in expectations, around half of the poorest students expect to go on to university at this age, a far bigger proportion than actually apply. So there appears to be no overall shortage of expectations in English secondary schools. The

[16] Steele, F., Vignoles, A., and Jenkins, A. (2007), 'The effect of school resources on pupil attainment: a multilevel simultaneous equation modelling approach', *Journal of the Royal Statistical Society*, Series A, 170 (3): 801–24. The authors find that between 14% and 22% of the variation in academic progress in secondary school is due to differences between schools as distinct from within schools. The proportion explained varies by subject.

[17] Anders, J. and Micklewright, J. (2013), 'Teenagers' expectations of applying to university: how do they change?' Department of Quantitative Social Science Working Paper 13-13, Institute of Education, University of London. See also Chowdry, H., Crawford, C., and Goodman, A. (2010), 'The role of attitudes and behaviours in explaining socio-economic differences in attainment at age 16', IFS Working Paper W10/15, London: Institute for Fiscal Studies.

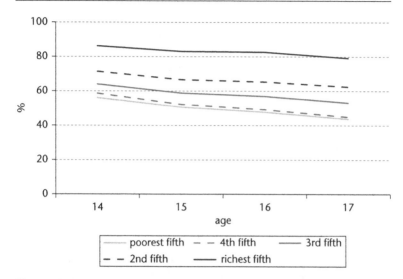

Figure 6.5. Young people in England who say they are 'very' or 'fairly' likely to apply to university (%), by fifths of the distribution of household income

Note: the data are drawn from the first Longitudinal Study of Young People in England (a sample of young people who were age 14 in the academic year 2003/4).

Source: Anders, J. and Micklewright, J. (2013), 'Teenagers' expectations of applying to university: how do they change?' Department of Quantitative Social Science Working Paper, UCL Institute of Education (Figure 7).

issue is translating these expectations into reality. For example, whilst nearly four fifths of those fourteen-year-olds who say they are 'very likely' to apply to university do actually make an application by age 20, this is less true of poor students. And as students move through their teenage years the percentage of young people saying that they are likely to go to university declines (as shown in Figure 6.5), and it declines more rapidly for those from poorer backgrounds. This means that the socio-economic gap in the percentage saying they are likely to apply to university widens as young people get older.

Even when considering expectations, however, attainment is key. What is most striking from the analysis of the survey data behind Figure 6.5 is that prior achievement, as measured by age 11 test scores, is a stronger predictor of students' university intentions than their socio-economic background. In particular, if a child comes from a low socio-economic group but also has high achievement at age 11, they are much more likely to say they will apply to university than a child from a high socio-economic group who has low achievement at age 11. Reassuringly, therefore, prior achievement appears to trump socio-economic background when it comes to determining students' expectations of going to university. Does this imply that expectations are not an issue? Not entirely. There is a group of initially high achieving poor students who do not expect to go to university, despite having the capability to do so. In fact, nearly a third of poor students who performed well on tests at age 11 did not say they were likely to apply to university, which may be a cause for concern.

Earlier in this chapter, we highlighted that non-school factors seem to be a bigger influence on pupils' achievement than the school they attend. Schools do, however, seem to affect students' expectations about going to university, even after allowing for differences in pupils' achievement. Whilst this evidence is indicative rather than conclusive, it does appear that schools, or perhaps specific teachers, are able to encourage some poor students to want to continue on to university. In other words they can influence pupils' expectations. This leaves an important question hanging, namely whether simply changing pupils' expectations can influence poor students' participation in higher education substantially, given that we know prior achievement is such a key determinant of whether students actually go to university. Our conclusion is that expectations matter at the margin and hence schools clearly have an important role here, as indeed may parents, and universities in their outreach work.

Thus, while we must not ignore the fact that prior achievement is the main driver of higher education participation decisions—and so efforts to improve poor children's achievement are critically important for reducing socio-economic gaps in access—there is reason to believe that prior attainment may not be the only barrier preventing some young people from poorer backgrounds from getting to (the highest status) universities. As we highlighted above, there are some children who were high achieving at the end of primary school who do not expect to go to university. There are also some young people with the GCSE and A-level grades to go to the highest status institutions who do not attend them.

For example, amongst state school students who took their A-levels in 2010, just 650 of those from the 20 per cent poorest families achieved at least 2 A grades in a 'facilitating' subject at A-level, compared with around 9,500 of those from the 20 per cent richest families. Even amongst students who achieved this high benchmark, 90 per cent of those from the richest fifth of families went on to attend one of the 41 high status institutions we have been considering throughout this book, compared to just under 86 per cent of those from the poorest fifth of families. Similar differences are apparent at other attainment levels too.

The large difference in attainment between those from richer and poorer families is clearly the biggest barrier to attending a high status institution, but these figures highlight that some small differences in participation remain even amongst those with the highest attainment. Of course the decision not to attend one of these high status institutions may be a rational choice for these students. But if there is a danger that some young people are not applying to high status institutions because they are not aware that they could do so, or they do not think they will get in, or they are not aware of the benefits of going, then this may be an area where better advice and guidance is needed.

The provision of accurate and up-to-date information on the costs and benefits of higher education has formed the basis of a number of interventions designed to 'widen' participation—a catch-all term that is often used to describe efforts to target groups who are currently under-represented in higher education. Some of these interventions have been shown to increase young people's knowledge of the costs and benefits of university, and have also raised their expectations of going, both of which have been found to be associated with higher university participation rates.[18]

Some more intensive strategies, such as attending a university 'summer school'—typically a period of a week or more that students spend on site at a particular university with other prospective students experiencing all aspects of university life, both academic and social, as well as receiving information about institution and subject choice and guidance on applications—have also been found to be effective at raising the application and participation rates of those from lower socio-economic backgrounds, especially to their host institutions. Indeed, this was thought to be one of the most effective elements of the national Aimhigher scheme, in operation during the 2000s, which was designed to provide co-ordinated outreach and career guidance to students from

[18] Interventions that have successfully increased knowledge of university costs and benefits include McGuigan, M., McNally, S., and Wyness, G. (2012), 'Student awareness of costs and benefits of educational decisions: Effects of an information campaign', Centre for the Economics of Education Discussion Paper 139, London School of Economics; Davies, P., Davies, N., and Qiu, T. (2016), 'Labour market knowledge and choice of school subject: A cluster randomised control trial with linked administrative data', forthcoming University of Birmingham Working Paper. Studies which have shown that expectations for university and knowledge of the graduate wage premium positively affect university attendance include Attanasio, O. and Kaufmann, K. (2009), 'Educational choices, subjective expectations and credit constraints', National Bureau for Economic Research Working Paper 15087, Cambridge, MA.

poor backgrounds to help them get to university, and was found to be effective in doing so on the basis of some evaluation evidence.[19]

While there are pockets of robust quantitative evidence on 'what works' to increase university access, many of the studies in this area have not used methodological approaches that are designed to elicit 'causal' estimates of their effect. (By this we mean we cannot be sure that changing the factors identified would necessarily *cause* university participation rates to increase, rather than simply being associated with higher participation for other reasons.) More evidence in this area would certainly be welcome, with a view to informing policymakers and practitioners about the types of policies that might be scalable, generalizable and successful in increasing participation rates amongst under-represented groups. The research presented in this chapter and the previous one suggests that long-term strategies which raise the school attainment of those from disadvantaged backgrounds may be the most successful at reducing socio-economic gaps in higher education participation in the long-term, but that increasing expectations and providing information to aid institution and subject choices, and strengthen university applications, might help in the meantime.

Summing Up

Over the last two chapters, we have shown that the key to successfully widening participation in higher education and improving access of poor students to high status universities is improvements in the achievement of these children in school. Much policy focus on widening participation is predicated on the idea that students' aspirations and knowledge of the higher education system are lacking, rather than their prior achievement. If, as we suggest here, the main reason for lower participation by poor students is their weak prior achievement, then such activities are unlikely to have a major impact on the proportions of

---

[19] For evidence on the effectiveness of summer schools, see, for example, Hefce (2010), 'Aimhigher summer schools: participants and progression to higher education', Higher Education Funding Council for England Issues Paper 2010/32; Hoare, T. and Mann, R. (2011), *The impact of the Sutton Trust's summer schools on subsequent higher education participation*, Report to the Sutton Trust. For evidence on the impact of Aimhigher on educational attainment and higher education participation rates, see Emmerson, C., Frayne, C., McNally, S., and Silva, O. (2005), *Evaluation of Aimhigher: Excellence Challenge: the early impact of Aimhigher: Excellence Challenge on pre-16 outcome: An economic evaluation*, Department for Education and Skills Research Report RR652; and Emmerson, C., Frayne, C., McNally, S., and Silva, O. (2006), *Aimhigher: Excellence Challenge: A policy evaluation using the Labour Force Survey*, Department for Education and Skills Research Report RR813.

poor students going to university. Overall, the main message from these chapters is that the key to success in terms of widening participation and ensuring better access of poor students to higher status universities is further work with the school system and with parents to raise the achievement levels of poorer students, particularly in early secondary school.

Part of the lower performance of students from poor backgrounds compared to their richer peers can be explained by the fact that pupils from different socio-economic backgrounds go to different secondary schools. Policies that aim to increase the quality of all secondary schools, particularly those attended by students from the poorest backgrounds, may therefore help to reduce the socio-economic gap in university attendance. Trying to reduce the sorting of pupils into schools on the basis of socio-economic background—to enable poorer pupils to access the best schools—may also help.

But we have also shown that there are substantial socio-economic differences in the likelihood of going to university even amongst pupils who attend the same secondary school, and we must further acknowledge that the drivers of these gaps go well beyond school walls. There are a range of non-school factors that affect the achievement and university participation decisions of pupils from different socio-economic backgrounds, and it can be challenging for policymakers to influence these factors.

This at least partially helps to explain the focus of efforts to reduce socio-economic gaps in university participation at school level. While there is little definitive evidence on which policies are best able to increase the participation rates of pupils from lower socio-economic backgrounds, the research summarized in this chapter provides some suggestions regarding the types of interventions that are likely to be most effective. For example, long-term interventions that aim to increase the achievement of poorer pupils in secondary school or even earlier are likely to be more effective than interventions that aim to tackle differences in the likelihood of applying (to a particular institution) amongst pupils with the requisite grades.

The last two chapters have highlighted that differences in achievement earlier in the school system are key to understanding socio-economic differences in the likelihood of going to university. Chapter 7 explores whether tackling these differences in achievement, thereby equipping more pupils from poorer backgrounds to go to university, is enough, or whether further socio-economic inequalities exist behind university doors as well.

7

Is Getting Pupils from Poorer Backgrounds through the Doors Enough?

So far in this book we have focused on understanding who gets to university. We have shown that how well young people do earlier in the school system plays a much more important role than either lack of aspirations or financial constraints in explaining why pupils from poorer backgrounds are so much less likely to go on to higher education than their richer counterparts. But, as we discussed in Chapter 1, the benefits of going to university accrue largely to those who have degrees, and in particular to those who attend high status institutions and graduate with the top degree classes. So, is getting to university really enough? Once there, do socio-economic differences in outcomes disappear or do they persist within university and beyond?

The *National Strategy for Access and Student Success in Higher Education*, published in 2014, emphasizes that 'widening participation' is about more than just access to university:[1]

> Our approach also recognises that widening participation should encompass the whole student lifecycle: preparing to apply and enter higher education; receiving study support and achieving successful completion; and progressing to postgraduate education or to/within employment.
>
> Foreword, *National Strategy*, April 2014

In this chapter we discuss the extent to which, even amongst the selected group of students who make it to university, there are socio-economic differences in the likelihood that they will drop-out, complete

---

[1] The strategy was published by the Department for Business, Innovation and Skills (BIS) in collaboration with the Office for Fair Access (OFFA) and the Higher Education Funding Council (Hefce), who are together responsible for distributing much of the funding and specifying much of the policy surrounding higher education (and in particular that on student access and progression) in England.

their degree, or graduate with a high degree class. (Chapter 8 discusses socio-economic differences in post-graduation outcomes.) We investigate how much of these gaps can be explained by differences in characteristics or exam results available on entry to university and how much remains unexplained, even amongst students studying the same subjects at the same universities. We also compare these findings by socio-economic background with results by the type of school a young person attended prior to entering higher education. One of the ways in which an individual's socio-economic background may affect their degree outcomes is via the type of school they attend. This, together with the fact that we observe next to no information about the socio-economic background of students who attended private schools, means it is of interest to compare how these individuals fare at university relative to others. One way to do this is a comparison of differences in outcomes by school type. The chapter concludes with some brief thoughts on the policy implications of our findings, which we pick up again in Chapter 9.

Socio-Economic Differences in Degree Outcomes

Most university courses in the UK last for three or four years, with performance assessed using 'degree classes' which reflect the average marks attained over the final one or two years of the course. The vast majority of students who start university in the UK end up graduating, with around 80 per cent of first degree entrants expected to complete their qualification, well above the OECD average of 70 per cent.[2] The dropout rate has not worsened appreciably over time either, despite the dramatic expansion of higher education.

UK universities set and mark their own exams, with final degree performance reflected in the award of one of five degree classes: the highest scoring students receive a 'first', followed by upper and lower second class degrees (2:1s and 2:2s), third class degrees and passes, with very few students failing to acquire enough marks to pass. There has been a dramatic rise in the proportion of students awarded the highest degree classes over the last 20 years, with the proportion getting firsts more than doubling (from just over 7 per cent to just under 18 per cent) and the proportion being awarded 2:1s increasing from 43 per cent to 50 per cent.[3] There is an ongoing debate about the extent to which these

---

[2] Table A4.1 of OECD Education at a Glance (2013).
[3] *Source*: HESA statistics: https://www.hesa.ac.uk/content/view/1973/239/.

rising grades reflect a genuine increase in the capacity of students and/or universities to deliver higher performance over time, or whether they (at least to some extent) represent grade inflation. What is clear is that the 'wage premium' paid to those with higher degree classes has held up well in spite of the increasing numbers of students receiving them, suggesting that employers are still willing to pay a premium for these graduates in the labour market.[4]

Thus, in spite of the increasing numbers of students going to university in the UK, average degree performance does not seem to have fallen, and indeed may even have risen. But the question remains as to whether degree performance differs by socio-economic background. Is it the case that poorer students are less likely to graduate, and if they complete their degrees, are less likely to be awarded the highest degree classes? To explore this, we return to the data described in earlier chapters, which enable us to follow pupils who go to school in England on to higher education anywhere in the UK. These data lend themselves to focusing on pupils born in a particular academic year and looking to see whether they start university at age 18 (straight after school) or age 19 (after a single gap year). We then follow these individuals through university, looking to see whether they drop out entirely (i.e. leave higher education completely, rather than transferring to another course or institution) in either their first or second year; whether they complete their degree within five years; and whether, conditional on graduating, they are awarded either a first or a 2:1.[5]

Figure 7.1 provides an overview of the socio-economic differences in these measures. Recall that our measure of socio-economic status when using these data is a combination of eligibility for free school meals and a series of measures of local area disadvantage. Figure 7.1 splits all state school pupils in England into 100 equally sized groups on the basis of this index of socio-economic status and plots the average outcome for each of these groups. The far left represents the 1 per cent least deprived state school students and the far right represents the 1 per cent most deprived state school students. It shows that degree outcomes vary substantially by socio-economic background. For example, less than 7 per cent of the least deprived state school students drop out of

---

[4] See, for example, Naylor, R., Smith, J., and Telhaj, S. (2016), 'Graduate returns, degree class premia and higher education expansion in the UK', *Oxford Economic Papers*, 68(2): 525–45.
[5] Degree completion and degree class outcomes focus on those studying full-time for first degrees in non-medical subjects. Drop-out focuses on individuals studying both full-time and part-time on any course.

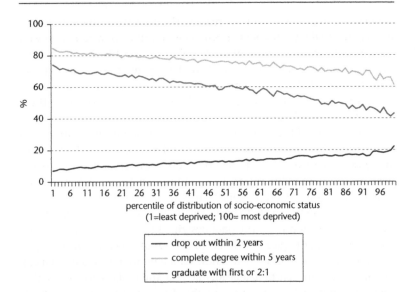

Figure 7.1. University students dropping out within 2 years, completing a degree within 5 years and graduating with a first or 2:1 (%), by socio-economic background

Note: individuals are classified as dropping out of university if they leave the sector entirely between the census taken in the year they enter university and the census taken two years later. Drop-out is calculated for state school students who sat their GCSEs between 2002 and 2006 and entered university at age 18 or age 19. Degree completion and degree class are constructed just for those who study full-time for a first degree in a non-medical subject, amongst state school students who sat their GCSEs between 2002 and 2004 and entered university at 18 or 19. Degree class is calculated amongst those who complete their degree within five years. The index of socio-economic status is calculated as described in Chapter 5.

Source: authors' calculations based on administrative data linking all pupils attending schools in England to all students attending universities in the UK.

university within two years, compared to more than 22 per cent of the most deprived state school students. Similarly, while nearly 85 per cent of the least deprived state school students complete their degree within five years and 74 per cent graduate with a first or a 2:1, the equivalent figures for the most deprived state school students are just 61 per cent and 43 per cent respectively.

English universities are not alone in seeing socio-economic differences in degree outcomes amongst their students: there are large gaps in the likelihood of graduation between those from rich and poor families in a range of other countries as well. For example, evidence from a survey of high school students in the USA suggests that, amongst those who attend the more selective four-year colleges, 73 per cent of students from the richest quarter of families go on to graduate compared with just 55 per cent of those from the poorest quarter of families.[6]

We showed earlier in this book that there are sizeable differences in terms of the likelihood of going to university (and to a high status institution) by socio-economic background. Our findings so far in this chapter suggest that, even amongst the relatively selected group of individuals who make it to university, there are further socio-economic differences in outcomes once at university. These differences are somewhat smaller in absolute terms than the gaps in participation, but they are nonetheless an important part of the story when thinking about the potential role for higher education as a vehicle for social mobility. It is therefore equally important from a policy perspective to consider what explains these differences in retention and progression by students' socio-economic background.

What Explains the Socio-Economic Differences in Degree Outcomes?

We saw in Chapter 5 that accounting for how well young people did in their exams at age 16 (at the end of compulsory schooling) explained pretty much all of the difference in university entry rates by socio-economic background. A key question is therefore whether differences in school attainment also help to explain why students from lower socio-economic backgrounds tend to perform less well at university than their richer counterparts.

Figure 7.2 illustrates this point, showing how the relationships between socio-economic status and drop-out, degree completion and degree class change as we account for the other ways in which young people from different socio-economic backgrounds differ from each other. Each bar summarizes the difference in degree outcomes between the 20 per cent most deprived state school pupils and the 20 per cent least deprived state school pupils. They are all in percentage point terms: they show how much more or less likely the richest fifth of pupils are to experience a particular outcome, on average, compared to the poorest fifth of pupils.

As we saw in Figure 7.1, there are large differences in degree performance between students from lower and higher socio-economic groups before accounting for any of the other ways in which these pupils differ.

---

[6] See, for example, Table 3.3 of Carnevale, A. and Rose, S. (2003), 'Socioeconomic status, race/ethnicity and selective college admissions', in Kahlenberg, R. (ed.), *America's Untapped Resource: Low-Income Students in Higher Education*, New York: The Century Foundation.

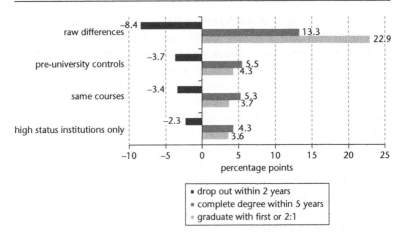

Figure 7.2. Differences (percentage points) in drop-out, degree completion and degree class between the richest and poorest fifth of state school students who go to university at age 18 or 19, controlling for different characteristics

Note: see the notes to Figure 7.1 for details of the sample and the definitions of socio-economic status, drop-out, degree completion, and degree class. The second set of bars adds controls for demographic and school characteristics measured at age 16, plus detailed measures of attainment at ages 11, 16, and 18. The third set of bars adds controls for course (institution times subject), plus whether the individual attended a university in the same region as they live. (The analysis of the determinants of drop-out decisions also controls for the type of qualification an individual is taking and whether they are studying full-time or part-time.) The final set of bars repeats the third set of bars for students attending one of the 41 high status institutions used throughout the book (i.e. it includes all other controls).

Source: Crawford, C. (2014), 'Socio-economic differences in university outcomes in the UK: drop-out, degree completion and degree class', Institute for Fiscal Studies Working Paper W14/31, London.

The first set of bars in Figure 7.2 shows that, relative to the 20 per cent most deprived pupils, the 20 per cent least deprived pupils are 8.4 percentage points less likely to drop out within two years (8.9 per cent compared to 17.3 per cent), 13.3 percentage points more likely to complete their degree within five years (81.7 per cent compared to 68.4 per cent) and 22.9 percentage points more likely to graduate with a first or 2:1 (70.1 per cent compared to 47.2 per cent).

The second set of bars shows what happens if we strip out any difference in degree outcomes that arises because the poorest fifth of pupils arrive at university 'looking' very different to the richest fifth of pupils. In essence it shows the average difference in degree outcomes that remains between the 20 per cent richest and 20 per cent poorest pupils after allowing for differences in students' characteristics (gender, ethnicity, age, month of birth and region) and their attainment prior to entering university (including at GCSE and A-level). We expected the length of these bars to shorten once we allowed for these differences and Figure 7.2 shows this to be the case. After accounting for students' characteristics and prior attainment, the difference in drop-out rates between those from the richest and poorest backgrounds approximately halves, falling to around 4 percentage points. Similarly, the difference in degree completion falls by around 60 per cent (to 5.5 percentage points) and the difference in the likelihood of getting a first or a 2:1 falls by about 80 per cent (to just over 4 percentage points).

This highlights that an important reason why poorer pupils have worse degree outcomes, on average, than their richer counterparts is because they tend to be less well-qualified on arrival at university. Indeed, lack of academic preparation is often highlighted as a major reason why students may under-perform at university.[7] But this is not the whole story: there are still large differences in outcomes by socio-economic background even after accounting for differences in all of these pre-university factors.

What could explain the remaining differences? The selection of young people from different socio-economic backgrounds into different universities or subjects may be one such explanation. We know that drop-out rates differ by institution and subject, with students studying at higher status institutions or for medicine and dentistry degrees, for example, less likely to drop out of university.[8] If students from poorer backgrounds are more likely to study at institutions or for subjects with higher drop-out rates, for whatever reason, then this might help to explain why their retention rates are lower than those from richer backgrounds.

The third set of bars in Figure 7.2 explores this possibility, comparing the outcomes of young people from the richest and poorest 20 per cent of families with the same prior attainment *and who attend the same university courses*. This also has the advantage of overcoming any concerns arising from the fact that it might be easier to obtain a high degree class at some universities or in some subjects than others. If the selection of young people from different socio-economic backgrounds into different degree courses were a key part of the reason why they end up with different degree outcomes, then we would expect to see the gap in

---

[7] For example, the National Audit Office—a body responsible for reviewing government spending and other government policies—suggested that entry qualifications were the strongest predictor of whether full-time students stayed in university or dropped out. See NAO (2007), *Staying the course: the retention of students in higher education*, Report by the Comptroller and Auditor General, London.

[8] See, for example, ibid.

outcomes fall markedly once we compare people attending the same courses. But this is not what we see: in fact, the differences in outcomes between the 20 per cent most and least deprived state school students are of similar magnitude whether we do or do not compare people on the same course. This suggests that the selection of young people from different backgrounds into different university courses provides only a very small part of the explanation for why they end up with different degree outcomes.

The fourth set of bars repeats the analysis shown in the third set of bars, but focuses just on students studying on the same degree courses within the group of forty-one high status universities used throughout the book. This helps us to understand whether the socio-economic gaps in degree outcomes are larger or smaller at different types of institutions. It shows that while the differences in outcomes between the most and least deprived state school students are slightly smaller, on average, at this group of high status institutions than they were for all universities, the differences do not fall to zero. Moreover, a similar picture holds in the USA, with socio-economic differences in graduation rates relatively consistent across more and less selective four-year colleges.[9] This suggests that the other factors that help to explain why students from poorer backgrounds do less well in their degrees than students from richer backgrounds are, to an extent, common across all universities, whether high status or otherwise, and whether in England or not. In other words, it is unlikely that differences in university policies and support explain the remaining differences in degree performance between more and less advantaged students; rather it is factors common to all universities.

What could these other factors be? There are a number of studies which consider the potential barriers faced by poorer students in terms of their continued participation and achievement in higher education.[10] These studies suggest that young people from higher socio-economic backgrounds experience fewer external pressures while studying than

[9] See, for example, Carnevale, A. and Rose, S. (2003), 'Socioeconomic status, race/ethnicity and selective college admissions', in Kahlenberg, R. (ed.), *America's Untapped Resource: Low-Income Students in Higher Education*, New York: The Century Foundation.

[10] Examples include Archer, L., Hutchings, M., and Ross, A. (2005), *Higher education and social class: issues of exclusion and inclusion*, Abingdon: Routledge; David, M., Bathmaker, A.-M., Crozier, G., Davis, P., Ertl, H., Fuller, A., Hayward, G., Heath, S., Hockings, C., Parry, G., Reay, D., Vignoles, A., and Williams, J. (eds) (2009), *Improving Learning by Widening Participation in Higher Education*, Abingdon: Routledge; Jones, R. (2008), *Student retention and success: a synthesis of research*, Higher Education Academy Report; Crosling, G., Heagney, M. and Thomas, L. (2009), 'Improving student retention in higher education', *Australian Universities Review*, 51: 9–18.

young people from lower socio-economic backgrounds; they also have access to greater levels of support. Both factors may help to explain their higher retention rates and achievement levels. For example, young people from poorer backgrounds are more likely to have to work in the labour market to support themselves (or their family) while they are studying, commitments which make it more difficult to study effectively. Students from richer families are also more likely to have access to a financial safety net than those from poorer families in the event of a financial shock, ensuring that students from wealthier backgrounds are less susceptible to dropping out of university because they cannot afford to continue.[11]

Another issue that is often put forward to help explain why those from lower socio-economic backgrounds may be more likely to drop out of university is social and cultural 'fit'. Sociological research points to the feelings of dislocation that some students from working class backgrounds feel when they enter higher education and the impact that this may have on their retention and achievement.[12] Economists, on the other hand, tend to view this issue through the lens of human capital theory, with differences in educational attainment, including at university level, being at least partly explained by differences in parental investments. These investments could be financial, educational or more general, giving rise to differences in skills which are not fully captured by their examination results which may influence their ability to succeed at university. For example, it may be that young people from richer backgrounds have greater resilience, motivation or independent study skills than those from poorer backgrounds, and that it is these unobserved 'non-cognitive' skills which lead to them having more positive degree outcomes. They may also have better knowledge of, or ability to access, support within or outside university to help overcome any challenges they may face that would otherwise knock them off course.[13]

---

[11] See, for example, Callender, C. and Kemp, M. (2000), *Changing student finances: Income, expenditure and the take-up of student loans among full-time and part-time higher education students in 1998–99*, DfEE Research Report 213, London: Department for Education and Employment; NAO (2007), *Staying the course: the retention of students in higher education*, Report by the Comptroller and Auditor General, London.

[12] See, for example, Reay, D., Crozier, G., and Clayton, J. (2010), '"Fitting in" or "standing out": working-class students in UK higher education', *British Educational Research Journal*, 36: 107–24.

[13] See, for example, Haveman, R. and Wolfe, B. (1995), 'The determinants of children's attainments: a review of methods and findings', *Journal of Economic Literature*, 33(4): 1829–78; Keane, M. and Wolpin, K. (2001), 'The effect of parental transfers and borrowing constraints on educational attainment', *International Economic Review*, 42: 1051–103.

Just as there is only limited robust empirical evidence on 'what works' to increase access to higher education for young people from lower socio-economic backgrounds, however, so there is relatively little 'causal' evidence about how to successfully intervene to increase retention, progression, and achievement once at university. Much of the evidence on these topics comes from qualitative research or from studies with no clear 'control' group, making it difficult to say what would have happened had the interventions not been carried out. Nonetheless, summaries of the latest evidence on this topic in England and elsewhere highlight a sense of 'belonging' as being particularly important in promoting student retention, with 'belonging' fostered by supportive peer relations, meaningful interaction between staff and students, and a teaching and learning environment with clearly defined goals and responsibilities that promotes students' confidence and knowledge.[14] Money worries do not feature prominently in summaries of the causes of university drop-out, and indeed there is mixed evidence on whether financial support in the form of bursaries helps promote retention and success in higher education.[15]

There does not seem to be only one type of intervention that successfully promotes 'belonging'. But the evidence suggests that such interventions should be mainstream (everyone should participate, rather than being restricted to small groups of at-risk students); proactive rather than reactive; and relevant to students (to foster engagement). Interventions at key transition times have been found to be particularly effective. For example, calling students prior to or close to course enrolment has been shown to reduce 'pre-entry' drop-out. Redesigning induction week events to foster greater peer interaction and small group work (with an academic purpose) has been found to reduce first year drop-out. The use of student 'ambassadors'—using older students to provide information, advice and guidance to newer students—has also been found to be effective. (This is also the case for

---

[14] See, for example, Tinto, V. (1987), *Leaving College: rethinking the causes and cures of student attrition*, Chicago: University of Chicago Press; Thomas, L. (2012), *Building student engagement and belonging in Higher Education at a time of change*, Final Report from the What Works? Student Retention and Success Programme, Paul Hamlyn Foundation, London.

[15] OFFA (2014), *Do bursaries have an effect on retention rates?* Interim Research Report 2014/02: Office for Fair Access, finds little evidence that bursaries significantly improve student retention, while Murphy, R. and Wyness, G. (2015), 'Testing means-tested aid', Centre for Economic Performance Discussion Paper 1396, London School of Economics, finds evidence that financial aid increases the likelihood of students graduating from university with a 'good' degree, by increasing both student retention and exam results.

interventions to encourage more young people from disadvantaged backgrounds to apply to university.)[16]

While this body of evidence provides some direction for policymakers and practitioners interested in promoting student retention and success, there is a clear need for more robust quantitative evidence of the effectiveness of such interventions. And showing how these policies work for different students in different settings—particularly whether they reduce socio-economic inequalities in outcomes—is an important area for future research.

How do these Findings Compare to those by School Type?

One of the ways in which an individual's socio-economic background may affect their degree outcomes is via the type of school they attend. This applies particularly when thinking about whether a pupil attends a private school: just 7 per cent of pupils in England do so at age 16 and, as we discussed earlier, these young people come, on average, from families with relatively high incomes. This may be one of the ways through which wealthier families are able to invest in their children. But even within the state sector, school type reveals something about a pupil's background, particularly when considering those attending selective state (grammar) schools.

As described in previous chapters, we do not have access to very rich information on socio-economic background in most of the administrative data that form the backbone of our knowledge in this area, and we observe no information whatsoever on pupils who attend private schools. We do, however, have information on the type of school attended and hence it is another interesting dimension of this picture of socio-economic differences in degree outcomes to consider whether they vary by school type.

We saw in Chapter 6 that the main way in which schools seem to influence whether or not a pupil goes to university is via their effect on a pupil's GCSE and A-level attainment. Here, we explore whether this is also the case for degree outcomes: how large are the differences in degree outcomes by school type, how much of this gap can we explain using

---

[16] See Thomas, L. (2012), *Building student engagement and belonging in Higher Education at a time of change*, Final Report from the What Works? Student Retention and Success Programme, Paul Hamlyn Foundation, London; Sutton Trust (2008), 'Increasing higher education participation amongst disadvantaged young people and schools in poor communities', Report to the National Council for Educational Excellence; Simpson, O. (2004), 'The impact on retention of interventions to support distance learning students', *Open Learning*, 19: 79–95.

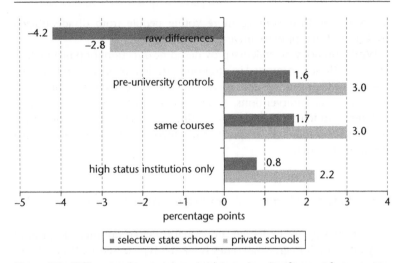

Figure 7.3. Differences (percentage points) in university drop-out between students who previously attended a selective state or private school at age 16 (relative to those attending non-selective state schools), controlling for different characteristics

Note: see the notes to Figure 7.1 for details of the sample and the definitions of socio-economic status and drop-out, and the notes to Figure 7.2 for the characteristics controlled for in each set of bars. Individuals are classified according to the school in which they sat their GCSEs (at the end of compulsory schooling at age 16). A selective school is one that formally admits pupils on the basis of academic achievement.

Source: authors' calculations based on administrative data linking all pupils attending schools in England to all students attending universities in the UK.

other characteristics—including prior attainment—and how much remains? This will provide an indication of the extent to which schools influence how well young people do once they enter university, over and above any effect they have on attainment. This could, for example, arise because of skills they have taught students, such as independent study or essay writing, or because of the social and cultural advantages that private or selective state schooling may confer.

Figures 7.3, 7.4 and 7.5 show, respectively, the average differences in the rates of drop-out, degree completion, and degree class between pupils who attended different secondary schools. Specifically, they show how these outcomes vary according to whether someone sat their GCSEs in a selective state (grammar) school or a private school, relative to a non-selective state school.

The first set of bars in each figure show, perhaps unsurprisingly, that students who previously attended a selective state or private secondary

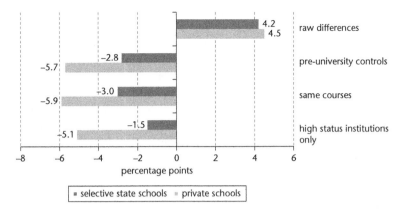

Figure 7.4. Differences (percentage points) in likelihood of completing degree between students who previously attended a selective state or private school at age 16 (relative to those attending non-selective state schools), controlling for different characteristics

Note: see the notes to Figure 7.1 for details of the sample and the definitions of socio-economic status and degree completion, and the notes to Figure 7.2 for the characteristics controlled for in each set of bars. Individuals are classified according to the school in which they sat their GCSEs (at the end of compulsory schooling at age 16). A selective school is one that formally admits pupils on the basis of academic achievement.

Source: authors' calculations based on administrative data linking all pupils attending schools in England to all students attending universities in the UK.

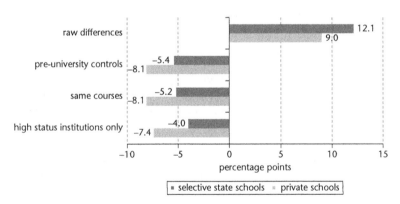

Figure 7.5. Differences (percentage points) in likelihood of graduating with first or 2:1 between students who previously attended a selective state or private school at age 16 (relative to those attending non-selective state schools), controlling for different characteristics

Note: see the notes to Figure 7.1 for details of the sample and the definitions of socio-economic status and degree class, and the notes to Figure 7.2 for the characteristics controlled for in each set of bars. Individuals are classified according to the school in which they sat their GCSEs (at the end of compulsory schooling at age 16). A selective school is one that formally admits pupils on the basis of academic achievement.

Source: authors' calculations based on administrative data linking all pupils attending schools in England to all students attending universities in the UK.

school have better outcomes at university, on average, than those who attended a non-selective state secondary school. For example, those who attended a private secondary school are, on average, 2.8 percentage points less likely to drop out within two years (Figure 7.3), 4.5 percentage points more likely to complete their degree within five years (Figure 7.4), and 9 percentage points more likely to graduate with a first or 2:1 compared to those who attended a non-selective state secondary school (Figure 7.5). Similarly, those who attended a selective state secondary school are 4.2 percentage points less likely to drop out, 4.2 percentage points more likely to complete their degree and 12.1 percentage points more likely to get a first or 2:1 than those who attended a non-selective state secondary school.

Once we account for student characteristics and measures of attainment observed prior to entering university (in the second set of bars in each of the three graphs), however, these patterns are reversed. Comparing pupils from similar backgrounds with the same prior attainment, those from private and selective state schools are now *more* likely to drop out, *less* likely to complete their degree and *less* likely to graduate with a first or 2:1 than those from non-selective state schools.[17] Moreover, these differences cannot be explained by students from different types of schools studying at different institutions or taking different subjects: they persist when we compare students on the same courses (in the third set of bars). For example, comparing students from the same backgrounds, with the same prior attainment and studying on the same courses, those who attended a private secondary school are, on average, 3 percentage points more likely to drop out, 5.9 percentage points less likely to complete their degree, and 8.1 percentage points less likely to graduate with a first or 2:1 compared to those who attended a non-selective state secondary school.

The differences between selective and non-selective state school students are smaller, but of the same sign. And a similar pattern of results is found if we compare pupils attending different schools on the basis of performance, such as the proportion of students in the school who achieve five A*–C grades at GCSE, or the extent to which their pupils' performance increases between age 11 and age 16. While those who attend higher-performing secondary schools have better university

---

[17] Similar results had previously been observed for private vs. state school students in terms of degree class. See, for example, Hefce (2005), 'Schooling Effects on Higher Education Achievement: Further Analysis—Entry at 19', Issues Paper no. 2005/09; Smith, J. and Naylor, R. (2001), 'Determinants of degree performance in UK universities: a statistical analysis of the 1993 student cohort', *Oxford Bulletin of Economics and Statistics*, 63: 29–60.

outcomes, on average, than those who attend lower-performing secondary schools, this is because they have higher attainment prior to university. The relationship is reversed once we compare pupils from similar backgrounds with similar measures of attainment.

The fact that accounting for differences in other characteristics between pupils attending different schools reverses the sign of these gaps stands in stark contrast to the results by socio-economic background (described above), where the gap between those from higher and lower socio-economic backgrounds was reduced but remained significant and, more importantly, of the same sign after accounting for the other ways in which these individuals differed. We end this chapter by considering what might help to explain these differing results and what implications for policy there might be.

Summing Up

This chapter has shown that, even amongst the selected group of young people who make it into higher education, those from poorer backgrounds are more likely to drop out, less likely to complete their degree and less likely to graduate with a first or 2:1 than those from richer backgrounds. If we combine these results with the findings about socio-economic differences in university entry in Chapter 5, then this implies that only around 8 per cent of state school students from the 20 per cent poorest families have completed a degree by their mid 20s, and only 4 per cent have graduated with a first or a 2:1. In comparison, amongst the 20 per cent richest state school students, 41 per cent will have a degree and around 30 per cent will have graduated with a first or 2:1. The socio-economic differences in higher education outcomes therefore compound the socio-economic differences in university entry to create large differences in graduation rates and degree performance between young people from different family backgrounds.

Three key results emerge from the analysis presented in this chapter. First, as was the case for university entry (and choice of institution) described in earlier chapters, differences in attainment prior to going to university play a key role in explaining why students from poorer backgrounds are more likely to drop out, less likely to complete their degree and more likely to graduate with a first or 2:1 than students from richer backgrounds. This suggests that an important part of any strategy to reduce socio-economic inequalities in degree acquisition and performance should be to increase the attainment of students from poor backgrounds earlier in the school system.

Second, the differences in degree outcomes between students from different socio-economic backgrounds that remain after controlling for prior attainment are apparent even between students studying on the same courses at the same universities, and they are evident at all universities. This suggests that the other factors at work that help to explain why students from poorer backgrounds do less well in their degrees are, to an extent, common across universities. This leaves open an important potential role for universities in providing additional support to students from lower socio-economic backgrounds to help increase retention and achievement at university, although clearly not all of the potential contributing factors may be fully mitigated by university action.

Third, there are systematic differences in degree performance for students who attended different types of schools, as well as between students from different socio-economic backgrounds. Interestingly, however, while we find that the relative under-performance of students from disadvantaged backgrounds remains after accounting for their characteristics and attainment on entry to university, the reverse is true for students from different schools. Comparing students with the same characteristics and the same exam results at ages 11, 16 and 18, our results suggest that students from non-selective (especially lower performing) state schools actually go on to outperform their counterparts from private and selective (or otherwise higher performing) state schools.

These results could be interpreted as suggesting that, amongst students with a given set of characteristics and measures of prior attainment, those from non-selective or lower-performing state schools have, on average, higher 'potential' to do well at university than those from selective (or otherwise high performing) state or private schools. This may, in turn, suggest that university entry requirements could be lowered for pupils from poorly-performing state schools in order to equalize the potential of all students being admitted to university. In other words, universities could 'contextualize' their entry offers on the basis of secondary school attended, in order to try and ensure that, at least on average, all students admitted to university are equally likely to complete their degrees and achieve similar degree classes, no matter which type of school they attended. Of course, not all pupils from low performing schools will go on to outperform pupils from high performing schools but our expectation based on these results is that they would do so on average. This would support 'contextualizing' admission decisions on the basis of school characteristics.

We do not see the same relative under-performance at the end of university amongst those from higher socio-economic backgrounds, however. Students from lower socio-economic backgrounds are still, on average, more likely to drop out, less likely to complete their degree and less likely to graduate with a first or 2:1 than those from higher socio-economic backgrounds, even once we compare individuals with the same characteristics and school exam results. In this situation it is not obvious that universities should make lower grade offers to disadvantaged students without providing additional support to ensure that they don't end up with weaker degree performance.

Of course, universities may want to use information on individuals' own socio-economic background to inform their admissions processes anyway. And in fact, our research suggests that they may already do so. Certainly, the data implies that poorer students who attend high status institutions have lower average GCSE and A-level attainment than their wealthier counterparts in the same institutions. For example, of those who enrol in one of our forty-one high status universities, 47 per cent of the most deprived students achieve at least three A or B grades at A-level, compared with 73 per cent of the least deprived students.[18] Even comparing students who attend the same courses, we still see some small differences, with those from higher socio-economic background outscoring those from lower socio-economic backgrounds by around 70 points on average (roughly equivalent to moving up two grades in one A-level). Of course this may suggest that universities are using contextualized admissions policies, or it may suggest that students from richer backgrounds exceed standard entry offers by more than those from poorer backgrounds because they tend to have higher grades on average. Nevertheless, our results suggest that it is more challenging for universities to identify prospective students from lower socio-economic backgrounds with strong potential to succeed and hence that they should not be expected to go on to outperform their richer peers, on average, at least not without additional support once at university.

The analysis presented in this chapter highlights that widening participation is not enough. Emphasis must also be placed on ensuring that young people from disadvantaged families, neighbourhoods, and schools are able to stay in university and perform to their potential, and, as we discuss in Chapter 8, that they have access to the same postgraduation study and employment opportunities as their more advantaged counterparts, in order to ensure that higher education is truly delivering equality of opportunity and outcomes.

[18] Crawford, C., Macmillan, L., and Vignoles, A. (2014), *Progress made by high-attaining children from disadvantaged backgrounds*, Social Mobility and Child Poverty Commission Research Report, June 2014.

8

Do Socio-Economic Differences Persist Beyond University?

There is a strong link between the socio-economic status of children and their parents. By this we mean that adults who grew up in poor families are less likely to be in work, less likely to work in professional jobs, and tend to have lower earnings than adults who grew up in richer families.[1] For example, children who grew up in one of the 20 per cent richest families in the early 1970s earn around twice as much at age 42 as children who grew up in one of the 20 per cent poorest families.[2] The evidence presented so far in this book suggests that differences in educational attainment might be one important for reason for this. Individuals from lower socio-economic backgrounds are much less likely to have gone to university and acquired a degree than their peers from higher socio-economic backgrounds. Given that we know having a degree tends to bring significant 'returns' (benefits) in the labour market—such as the ability to work in more appealing occupations or to earn more—these socio-economic differences in university access may explain at least part of the reason why those from lower socio-economic backgrounds tend to earn less than their peers who grew up in richer families.

[1] See, for example, Erikson, R. and Goldthorpe, J. (1992), *The Constant Flux: A Study of Class Mobility in Industrial Societies*, Oxford: Oxford University Press; Blanden, J., Goodman, A., Gregg, P., and Machin, S. (2004), 'Changes in Intergenerational Mobility in Britain', in Corak, M. (ed.), *Generational Income Mobility in North America and Europe*, Cambridge: Cambridge University Press; Macmillan, L. (2014), 'Intergenerational worklessness in the UK and the role of local labour markets', *Oxford Economic Papers*, 66: 871–89.

[2] These figures are based on the same survey of individuals born in 1970 that is described later in the chapter. It uses measures of family income at age 10 that were created as part of the Cohort and Longitudinal Studies Enhancement Resources (CLOSER) grant awarded by the Economic and Social Research Council. We thank Chris Belfield and Ellen Greaves at the Institute for Fiscal Studies for producing these measures.

Research supports this hypothesis, suggesting that how well people did in exams at ages 16 and 18 (which we showed in Chapter 5 to be crucial determinants of university access), and in higher education, can together explain about one third of the link between the income of parents and the earnings of their sons (the research did not include daughters).[3] In other words, once we compare individuals with the same educational attainment, the relationship between their family's socio-economic status and their own labour-market success should be much lower: we expect education to 'level the playing field'.

But is this what education and, in particular, higher education actually does? In this chapter we document differences in labour market outcomes, including access to 'top jobs' and earnings, between graduates from different socio-economic backgrounds, showing that those from poorer families do indeed have worse outcomes, on average, than their richer peers. We then go on to explain why this might be. We saw in Chapters 4 and 5 that young people from disadvantaged backgrounds are less likely to go to high-status institutions and in Chapter 7 that they are less likely to obtain the highest degree classes. Because of the differences in degree 'returns' by institution and degree class that we reported in Chapter 1, we might expect this to explain part of the reason why graduates from lower socio-economic backgrounds earn less than their richer peers. But is this the whole story? We investigate to what extent these different degree choices and outcomes lead to differences in post-graduation labour market success, and to what extent occupation and earnings differ by socio-economic background even amongst students studying the same subjects at the same institutions and who get the same degree classes. In doing so, our goal is to try to understand the extent to which increasing participation, retention and performance at university is sufficient for higher education to act as an 'engine of social mobility', or whether there is more work to be done to ensure equal opportunities after graduation as well.

Socio-Economic Differences in Labour Market Outcomes

In contrast to the rich administrative data available to study the determinants of university entry and performance in England (used extensively in the past few chapters), the data available to explore the

---

[3] Blanden, J., Gregg, P., and Macmillan, L. (2007), 'Accounting for intergenerational income persistence: noncognitive skills, ability and education', *The Economic Journal*, 117: C43–C60.

determinants of post-graduation outcomes are relatively poor or at least they have been until recently. We must therefore piece together a picture of the differences in occupations and earnings between graduates from different socio-economic backgrounds soon after graduation and through their working lives from a variety of sources.

The best source of information on labour market outcomes soon after graduation comes from a survey of UK university leavers.[4] All those who graduate from university are asked to complete a questionnaire about their current labour market activities six months after leaving, with around 80 per cent of UK students responding each year. Every other year, a subset of those who responded to the six-month survey are asked similar questions a further three years down the line. We focus on the outcomes at the three-and-a-half-year follow-up, as six months after graduation is rather early to consider whether individuals have successfully transitioned into the labour market. Using these data, we can understand whether individuals went into a 'top job'—which we define as a professional or higher managerial occupation—and indeed how much they earned if they were in work.[5]

The measures of socio-economic status available in these data are relatively weak. Respondents are asked to provide information on their parents' occupations, from which we could deduce whether they were in professional or managerial occupations, for example, but nearly 30 per cent of individuals do not answer this question, and we may furthermore have concerns about how accurately graduates are able to report their parents' jobs. We therefore focus instead on how outcomes differ according to the type of school attended immediately prior to going to university—specifically, by whether the individual attended a state or a private school.[6] This information is still missing for around 18 per cent of graduates, but may be recalled with greater accuracy than parental occupation. Around 12 per cent of graduates are recorded as attending a private school in these data. (This is higher than the

---

[4] These are the 'Destinations of Leavers from Higher Education' data collected by the Higher Education Statistics Agency.

[5] The findings on 'top jobs' in this chapter come from Macmillan, L., Tyler, C., and Vignoles, A. (2014), 'Who gets the top jobs? the role of family background and networks in recent graduates' access to high-status professions', *Journal of Social Policy*, 44: 487–515. The findings on earnings at this point in time come from Crawford, C. and Vignoles, A. (2014), 'Heterogeneity in graduate earnings by socio-economic background', IFS Working Paper W14/30, London: Institute for Fiscal Studies.

[6] We are unable to separate state schools into those that do and do not select pupils on the basis of academic attainment, as we did in Chapter 7. It should also be noted that the analysis in Chapter 7 compared pupils on the basis of the type of school they attended at age 16 (where they sat their GCSEs or equivalent qualifications), while the data here relates to the type of school attended at age 18 (for A-levels or equivalents).

proportion of the school population who attend private school because, as we saw in Chapter 5, private school students are more likely to go to university than their state school counterparts.)

We use data on UK domiciled students under the age of 25 who graduated from university in July 2007. (The three-and-a-half-year follow-up survey therefore took place in January 2011.) We find that graduates who went to private schools are, on average, 9.5 percentage points more likely to be in a 'top job' than graduates who went to state schools three and a half years after leaving university. This is a sizeable difference, given that around 30 per cent of all graduates went into these occupations. Amongst those in work, in any type of job, private school graduates also earn around £4,500 more per year, on average, than those who attended state schools—equivalent to a 'premium' of around 17 per cent.[7]

This suggests that there are substantial differences in outcomes, on average, between those who went to state and private schools three and a half years after graduation. But perhaps a more pressing policy question is whether these early gaps persist, entrenching socio-economic differences in labour market outcomes throughout individuals' working lives, or whether those from lower socio-economic backgrounds or state schools catch up with their peers from higher socio-economic backgrounds or private schools as they gain more experience or employers learn more about their skills.

To do so, we must of course look further back in time, comparing the outcomes of graduates who left university a larger number of years ago. We use two additional data sources for this analysis. Some of us have been fortunate to be amongst the first researchers to have access to administrative data on all students who borrowed money from the government in order to help meet the costs of their tuition fees and living expenses whilst at university. These data were linked to tax records, providing details of the taxable income of student loan borrowers from the time of graduation until the 2012/13 tax year. Using data on students who took out loans in 1999, we were able to compare the taxable incomes of those from the 20 per cent richest families with the taxable incomes of all other students a decade after leaving university. In doing so, we found that women from the highest income families

---

[7] Other authors have also identified differences in earnings between state and private school students. See, for example, Green, F., Machin, S., Murphy, R., and Zhu, Y. (2012), 'The changing economic advantage from private schools', *Economica*, 79: 658–79; Broughton, N., Ezeyi, O., Hupkau, C., Keohane, N., and Shorthouse, R. (2014), *Open Access: An Independent Evaluation*, Social Market Foundation Report to the Sutton Trust.

earned 24 per cent more than those from poorer families. In the case of men, the figure was even higher, at around 30 per cent.[8]

Such socio-economic differences persist deeper into adulthood as well. Using data from a survey of all babies born in Great Britain during a particular week of April 1970, we can look at graduates' earnings in mid-career, at age 42, again finding evidence of non-negligible socio-economic gaps.[9] For example: graduates whose father worked in a higher managerial or professional occupation at age 10 earn around 7 per cent more than those whose father worked in any other occupation; those who grew up in the fifth highest income families earn around 10 per cent more than those who grew up in poorer families; and those whose mother had A-level qualifications or above earn around 9 per cent more than those whose mother had any lower qualifications.

Are we Comparing Like with Like?

The previous section showed clearly that there are socio-economic differences in labour market outcomes that emerge shortly after graduation and seem to persist for at least 20 years. On the basis of this evidence alone, it would seem that higher education does not fully 'level the playing field'. But of course we know that the characteristics, skills and experiences of those who make it to university differ by socio-economic background. We have already shown that individuals from lower socio-economic backgrounds are less likely to go to the highest status universities and are less likely to graduate with the top degree classes. We have also shown that, even amongst those who make it to university, students from lower socio-economic backgrounds have lower school exam results, on average, than those from higher socio-economic background. If these measures of attainment also affect an individual's chances of moving into a professional occupation or of being paid more

[8] As we discussed in Chapter 3, the amount that students can borrow from the government depends on their parents' income. Those with gross incomes above a threshold (approximately £35,000–41,000 per year depending on the year of study) could only borrow up to a certain amount. By identifying students borrowing exactly this amount in the data, we could identify students from higher income households. Using this method, approximately 20% of the cohort is identified as being from a higher income family. These results are from Britton, J., Dearden, L., Shephard, N., and Vignoles, A. (2016), 'How English domiciled graduate earnings vary with gender, institution, subject and socio economic background', IFS Working Paper W16/06, London: Institute for Fiscal Studies. They refer to differences in median earnings.
[9] The findings on earnings at age 42 come from Crawford, C. and van der Erve, L. (2015), 'Does Higher Education Level the Playing Field? Socio-Economic Differences in Graduate Earnings', *Education Sciences*, 5: 380–412.

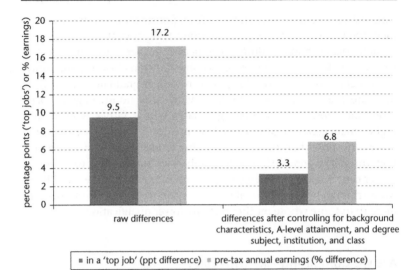

Figure 8.1. Differences (percentage points or %) in labour market outcomes three and a half years after graduation between students who previously attended state and private schools

Note: the bars show how much more likely a graduate who previously attended a private school is to achieve the outcome than a graduate who previously attended a state school. The differences in the likelihood of being in a 'top job' are in percentage point (ppt) terms (e.g. if 40% of private school students are in a 'top job' compared to 30% of state school students then the difference would be 10 percentage points). The differences in earnings are in % terms. The analysis is based on self-reported occupation and pre-tax annual earnings for a subset of graduates in work three and a half years after leaving university in July 2006/7. Students are grouped according to the last school they attended before entering university.

Sources: the findings on 'top jobs' come from Macmillan, L., Tyler, C., and Vignoles, A. (2014), 'Who gets the top jobs? The role of family background and networks in recent graduates' access to high-status professions', *Journal of Social Policy*, 44: 487–515. The findings on earnings come from Crawford, C. and Vignoles, A. (2014), 'Heterogeneity in graduate earnings by socio-economic background', Institute for Fiscal Studies Working Paper W14/30.

later in life, then they might also help to explain the differences in labour market performance. So the question remains: is there parity of outcomes amongst *equivalently qualified* graduates from different backgrounds?

The short answer is, 'No'. Returning to the data on labour market performance three and a half years after graduation, Figure 8.1 shows how much more likely graduates who previously attended private schools are to be in a 'top job' (the dark grey bars) and how much more they earn (the light grey bars) than graduates who previously attended state schools. The first set of bars represents the raw differences in outcomes described above, showing that graduates from private schools are 9.5 percentage points more likely to be working in a professional or higher managerial occupation, and earn around 17 per cent more (in any job), on average, than graduates from state schools.

The second set of bars shows that happens when we account for the other ways in which graduates who attended different schools differ from each other. In particular, we account for differences in other factors evident prior to entering university, including gender, ethnicity, neighbourhood measures of deprivation and A-level attainment, and in what and where individuals studied and how well they did at university, by accounting for degree subject, institution and class. These factors help to explain a substantial proportion of the differences in occupation and earnings that we observe between graduates from different schools, with the remaining unexplained gap in outcomes falling by around two thirds (to just over 3 percentage points) when focusing on occupation and by just under half (to just under 7 per cent) when considering earnings.

These remaining unexplained differences—the reasons why graduates from private schools have better jobs or earn more than graduates from state schools—are not negligible. They suggest, for example, that even comparing graduates who studied the same subjects at the same universities with the same levels of attainment, those from private schools still earn, on average, around 7 per cent more than their state school counterparts. This is similar in magnitude to the earnings premium associated with achieving a first class degree or a 2:1 relative to a lower degree class, for example.[10]

Moreover, the difference in earnings cannot be explained by the fact that those from private schools are more likely to go into potentially higher paying jobs. Even comparing those who are similar in all other respects *and* who went into similar occupations after leaving university, graduates from private schools still earn around 6 per cent more, on average, than graduates from state schools. (This is equivalent to around £1,500 per year in our data.) This suggests that the channelling of private school students into high status professions is not the main reason why they earn more than their state school counterparts. Instead, similarly qualified state and private school graduates who enter the same occupations seem to earn different salaries.

The same is also true if we focus on earnings later in life. For example, using the tax records of students who borrowed money from the government to fund their undergraduate studies and comparing students

---

[10] See, for example, Naylor, R., Smith, J., and Telhaj, S. (2016) 'Graduate returns, degree class premia and higher education expansion in the UK', *Oxford Economic Papers*, 68(2): 525–45.

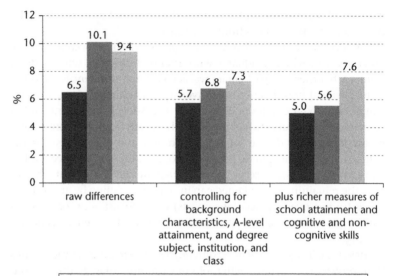

Figure 8.2. Differences (%) in annual pre-tax earnings at age 42 between graduates from different socio-economic backgrounds

Notes: analysis based on a survey of individuals born in a particular week of April 1970 who were in work at age 42 (in 2012). Bars show the % difference in pre-tax annual earnings between individuals from different socio-economic backgrounds.

Source: Crawford, C. and van der Erve, L. (2015), 'Does higher education level the playing field? Socio-economic differences in graduate earnings', *Education Sciences*, 5: 380–412.

who went to the same university and studied the same subject, graduates from higher income backgrounds still earn around 10 per cent more than those from lower income backgrounds a decade after leaving university.[11] And Figure 8.2 returns to the survey data for individuals born in April 1970, comparing the differences in earnings at age 42 between graduates whose father worked in a higher managerial or professional occupation at age 10 (compared to any other occupation); between those who grew up in a family with one of the 20 per cent highest incomes (compared to those who grew up in poorer families); and between those whose mother has A-level qualifications or above (compared to any lower qualifications).

---

[11] See Britton, J., Dearden, L., Shephard, N., and Vignoles, A. (2016), 'How English domiciled graduate earnings vary with gender, institution, subject and socio economic background', IFS Working Paper W16/06, London: Institute for Fiscal Studies.

The first set of bars shows the raw differences in earnings described above. The second set of bars shows the differences after accounting for the same types of characteristics we accounted for in the three-and-a-half year follow-up data—namely, gender, ethnicity, region and type of school attended, number of A-levels, and degree class, subject, and institution. They show that we can again explain some, but not all, of the gap in earnings by socio-economic background. For example, similarly qualified graduates whose father worked in a higher managerial or professional occupation when they were age 10 continue to earn around 6 per cent more at age 42 than those whose father worked in any other occupation. While the gaps by family income and mother's education fall slightly once we include these controls, those who grew up in the 20 per cent highest-income families still earn around 7 per cent more than those who grew up in poorer families, while those whose mother has A-level qualifications or above earn around 7 per cent more, on average, than those whose mother has any lower qualifications.

What Might Explain the Remaining Differences in Labour Market Outcomes?

So what else could explain these differences in labour market outcomes between equivalently qualified graduates from similar backgrounds who studied the same subjects at the same universities and achieved the same degree classes? It does not seem to be the result of an 'old boys' network', at least not on the basis of the latest quantitative research. Accounting for how graduates got their jobs—whether they were recommended by friends or family, for example—does not seem to explain the differences.[12] Some of the other potential explanations are similar to those put forward to explain the differences in degree performance by socio-economic background in Chapter 7. It could, for example, be that we are not able to capture well enough the differences in skills that graduates from different socio-economic backgrounds possess on leaving university. If those from higher socio-economic backgrounds (or who attended private schools) had better cognitive or non-cognitive skills than their poorer (state school) peers, then the fact that we do not account for these factors may bias our results, leading us to believe that those from

---

[12] See, for example, Macmillan, L., Tyler, C., and Vignoles, A. (2014), 'Who gets the top jobs? the role of family background and networks in recent graduates' access to high-status professions', *Journal of Social Policy*, 44: 487–515.

different socio-economic backgrounds are benefiting differentially from going to university, when in fact the differences in outcomes arise simply because they have different types or levels of skills, which employers reward.

We are lucky in the UK to have very rich information on children who have been followed since birth as part of various national surveys. As well as labour market outcomes at age 42, the study that has followed the children born in April 1970 that we described earlier also collected a set of measures of cognitive and non-cognitive skills during childhood, plus detailed information on school qualifications and grades. As we saw in Chapter 5, rich measures of attainment at the end of compulsory schooling were able to explain all of the gap in university access between pupils from the 20 per cent richest and 20 per cent poorest backgrounds, so they might also help to explain the remaining socio-economic differences in post-graduation labour market outcomes. A similar rationale can be put forward for why we should include measures of cognitive and non-cognitive skills as well.

The third set of bars in Figure 8.2 shows what effect adding these characteristics has on estimates of the remaining socio-economic differences in graduate earnings. The answer is not much, and certainly not enough to explain away the differences in earnings entirely. Hence this evidence confirms the tenor of our earlier findings, namely that socio-economic gaps in graduates' labour market outcomes persist well beyond university and cannot be entirely accounted for by differences in characteristics, skills and experience on graduation.

What's left that could help to explain the remaining differences? Well, it could be other things that happen after graduation with an undergraduate degree, in which there are socio-economic gradients and which also matter for earnings. One example could be the acquisition of postgraduate qualifications. The proportion of the population aged 20–60 with postgraduate qualifications has almost tripled over the last 20 years, from around 4 per cent of workers in the mid-1990s to 11 per cent by 2011, but the 'return' that workers with postgraduate qualifications receive relative to those with undergraduate qualifications has also risen, from around 7 per cent to around 13 per cent over the same time period. If there are socio-economic differences in access to postgraduate education, then this could help to explain the differences in earnings later in life.

Inequalities in access to postgraduate education are indeed substantial, with individuals who grew up in one of the richest 20 per cent of families over four times more likely to have a postgraduate degree than those who grew up in one of the poorest 20 per cent of families

(3 per cent vs. 13 per cent).[13] In fact, Alan Milburn, the government's Independent Reviewer on Social Mobility and Child Poverty, said in a report in 2012 that 'lack of access to postgraduate study is in danger of becoming a social mobility time bomb' and there have since been moves to introduce government support for some students undertaking post-graduate study, where—in contrast to the situation for undergraduate higher education—fees are unregulated and must be paid up-front.[14] But despite these significant differences in both access and returns to postgraduate study, accounting for whether the graduates in our data have obtained a postgraduate qualification actually explains very little of the reason why they go on to earn more later in life, with the gaps shown in the third set of bars in Figure 8.2 remaining virtually unchanged compared to the second set.

Is it Worth Individuals from Poor Backgrounds Going to University?

The analysis presented so far in this chapter suggests that graduates from lower socio-economic backgrounds are getting a raw deal from their investment in higher education: despite the fact that they have similar skills and qualifications, they seem to earn less, on average, than gradu-ates from higher socio-economic backgrounds. Does this mean that it is not worth them going to university at all? That is definitely not the case. It all depends who we compare them to.

To understand how much people benefit from going to university, the standard approach taken compares those who go with a similar group of individuals with the qualifications to go but who for some reason did not do so. In the case of higher education in England, this has typically meant focusing on individuals with at least two or more A-level passes, comparing the outcomes of those who go to university with the out-comes of those who do not. To understand whether the benefits of

---

[13] Lindley, J. and Machin, S. (2012), 'The quest for more and more education: implications for social mobility', *Fiscal Studies*, 33: 265–86.

[14] In response to these concerns, the Government has announced that income-contingent loans of up to £10,000 will be available to Masters students from 2016/17. These will be available on similar terms to the undergraduate loans discussed at length in Chapter 3, except that payments will be made at a rate of 6% of income above the threshold of £21,000 per year (as outlined in the government's response to the consultation on support for postgraduate study published in November 2015). The reference to a 'social mobility time bomb' is made in *University Challenge: How Higher Education Can Advance Social Mobility*, A progress report by the Independent Reviewer on Social Mobility and Child Poverty, October 2012.

going to university are larger or smaller for those from different socio-economic backgrounds, we can repeat this exercise for different groups of individuals and compare the results. In other words, we can compare those from lower socio-economic backgrounds with two or more A-level passes who do and don't go to university and see what the difference is, and separately compare those from higher socio-economic backgrounds with two or more A-level passes who do and don't go to university and see what the difference is for them. Then we can compare these two differences to see which is bigger. Is it more beneficial for those from higher socio-economic backgrounds to go to university (relative to having two or more A-levels), or is it more beneficial for those from lower socio-economic backgrounds to go (relative to having two or more A-levels)?

We have undertaken these calculations for individuals at age 42 using the same data on those born in 1970 that we have used elsewhere in the chapter. The results suggest that, amongst those who grew up in the richest half of families, individuals who went to university earn, on average, 10 per cent more than their counterparts from similar backgrounds but who left education after taking A-levels. The equivalent figure for those who grew up in the poorest half of families is 20 per cent. In other words, the benefit of going to university amongst those from poorer families is about double what it is for those from richer families. Thus while it doesn't look like graduates from lower socio-economic backgrounds earn quite as much as similarly qualified graduates from higher socio-economic backgrounds—a fact which clearly needs to be addressed—it does appear that going to university is still a good investment, on average, for those from lower socio-economic backgrounds.[15]

Summing Up

In this chapter we have explored what happens to graduates from different socio-economic backgrounds after they leave university. We have shown that there are quite stark differences in postgraduate progression and labour market success between those from more and less advantaged backgrounds. Most of these differences can be explained by

---

[15] These figures are lower than the average return of 27% cited in Chapter 1 because we are able to account for more of the ways in which individuals who did and did not go to university differ in this data than was possible in the data used to calculate the 27% figure. The 27% figure also represents an average across earnings of graduates and non-graduates at all ages, while these estimates focus just on individuals at age 42 in 2012.

differences in graduates' prior attainment, a recurring theme throughout this book. This, as ever, points to the importance of improving the school achievement of students from lower socio-economic backgrounds in order to increase their life chances. However, what is notable is that differences in earnings across socio-economic groups do remain even after accounting for differences in graduates' characteristics and attainment, both before and during university. These differences are not easily explainable by the other ways in which graduates from different socio-economic backgrounds differ from each other, at least not based on the things that we can capture in rich survey data. For example, the remaining gaps cannot be explained by differences in an extensive range of cognitive or non-cognitive skills, or because of differences in networks which may enable graduates from richer backgrounds to find (high paying) jobs more easily than graduates from poorer backgrounds.

It is clearly important from a policy perspective to understand why graduates from lower socio-economic backgrounds do not seem to reap the same rewards from similar university experiences as their richer peers. At the same time, however, it is important to remember that those from lower socio-economic backgrounds do still benefit from going to university, on average, if we compare them to equivalently qualified individuals from similar backgrounds who do not go. In a sense this brings us back to the fundamental importance of ensuring that individuals from poorer backgrounds can get to university in the first place, and it is to some suggestions of how this issue—and others raised throughout the book—could be addressed that we now turn.

9

What Do We Conclude?

In this book we have summarized the latest evidence for England on the magnitude and drivers of the long standing differences in university entry between young people from richer and poorer backgrounds, discussing potential barriers arising from lack of finance, aspirations, and achievement. We have also shed some much needed light on how well students from different backgrounds do once they arrive at university and indeed after they leave, finding that focusing interventions solely on getting more poor children through the doors of higher status universities is unlikely to be enough for higher education to truly 'level the playing field' between those from different backgrounds.

In this chapter we highlight the implications of the key points made throughout the book for the main stakeholders who have an interest in higher education: the government; universities; and students and their families. We do not rehearse in detail the findings from each chapter but rather focus on the meaning of the results for policy. We note again at this point that we have not considered all aspects of higher education and, in particular, we have focused on the socio-economic differences evident amongst young people going to university to study full-time. We have not dwelt on the important issues faced by mature and part-time students, nor at length on the issues of differential access to postgraduate study. Nor have we considered differences in university access and outcomes on the basis of other characteristics, such as gender, ethnicity or disability. Our findings should nevertheless be useful for those involved in undergraduate higher education, providing a better understanding of the drivers of the large socio-economic inequalities evident in the system and hence how best to address them.

How Important is the Issue of University Funding?

As outlined in Chapter 3, England has undergone a major reform to its funding of higher education in recent years, moving from a system of grants paid directly by the government to universities accompanied by relatively low student fees, to one in which grants have been dramatically reduced and replaced by much higher tuition fees. At the same time, upfront support to help students meet their living expenses has risen, but all government support now comes in the form of loans (which must be repaid) rather than grants (which do not).

These changes were introduced against a backdrop of considerable uncertainty over their likely effects on university entry, particularly on those from poorer families. To date, however, there is little sign that they have negatively affected overall entry to university or entry amongst students from disadvantaged backgrounds, at least amongst the group of young full-time students that have been the focus of this book. Indeed, as we showed in Chapter 4, participation in higher education has continued to rise, and more so amongst those from the poorest neighbourhoods. While we do not know how much more strongly university entry might have risen had tuition fees not increased, demand seems to have held up well so far.

One likely reason for the relatively benign effects on university access is that the fees charged to students in England do not have to be paid up-front. Instead, all students, regardless of family income, can borrow money from the government to cover their fees (and a contribution towards their living costs). These loans do not have to be repaid until after graduation, and only once income rises above a certain amount per year. Eventually, any outstanding debt is written off. These 'income-contingent' loans play a crucial role in insuring those going to university against paying a high price for their university education if they go on to earn relatively little (achieve poor returns) in the future, thus taking some of the risk out of the decision to go to university in the first place.

The fact that participation does not appear to have fallen so far suggests that students and their parents must have a reasonably good understanding of the student support system, despite the negative press coverage which these changes have generally received. Certainly, a lot of work has gone into ensuring that prospective students understand that 'income contingent' loans are fundamentally different from bank loans or credit card debts and so do not need to be faced with the same kind of trepidation. However, as we noted in Chapter 3, there is clearly more that could be done. Universities, in particular, need to do more to make clear the financial support they offer (in the form of bursaries and fee waivers) *before* the point at which students make their application decisions in order for these types of support to realistically affect university access. Efforts to promote understanding of both government and university support will doubtless need to continue, especially if the generosity of the system is reduced further in future.

At the time of writing, in early 2016, the loan repayment terms that students face mean that many of them are unlikely to repay their loans in full. This means that the 'sticker price' of a university education—fees of £9,000 per year for most students, plus additional living expenses—is somewhat higher than the true cost that is likely to be paid in many cases. This is, however, a relatively risky way of delivering a public subsidy for higher education if there is a chance that at least some students are averse to taking on debt. Many will be faced with very large debts at the end of their university education, running into the mid tens of thousands of pounds. While income-contingent loans should not be viewed in the same way as other types of debt, those who started university after 2012 have only just graduated, and we do not yet know whether these debts may affect other aspects of their lives as well (such as labour supply or savings choices, or whether banks might start taking them into account when making mortgage decisions).

This may be of particular concern if students from poorer families are more likely to be affected than students from richer families. The student loan system is broadly progressive if we think about how much individuals end up paying for their education compared to how much they earn over their lifetimes. Those who benefit the least from their university education (who go on to have low earnings) are likely to end up repaying the least, while those with higher earnings are likely to repay more.

But it is less clear how the cost of going to university varies with family income. As of 2016/17, it is certainly the case that if students take out the full amount of the loans to which they are entitled, then those from the poorest families will end up with the highest debts, because they are entitled to borrow more to help cover their living costs. But, as we have shown in Chapter 8, these individuals also have a higher chance of ending up as lower earners, so they may be relatively unlikely to repay these larger loans in full.

What is clear is that the current incarnation of the student loan system still provides a large degree of public subsidy for higher education, meaning that the public cost of higher education rises for every student who goes. This is particularly pertinent bearing in mind the government's recent removal of the cap on student numbers, enabling universities to recruit as many students as they wish onto their undergraduate courses. The government may therefore face calls to tweak the parameters of the existing loan system or to take more radical action to combat an increase in the level of public subsidy of higher education in future.

How could this be done, while still ensuring that young people from poorer families are not put off entering higher education? This will be a difficult balancing act. At a minimum, any changes need to avoid significant upfront costs for students, as this would almost certainly reduce the numbers of children from poorer families who end up going to university. It would also seem sensible for the government not to retrospectively change the loan repayment terms for those who have already taken out loans, as they have recently shown themselves willing to do, as this added uncertainty over the amount students will have to repay in future may undo some of the insurance value offered by income-contingent loans.

It is also, as yet, uncertain how plans for a 'Teaching Excellence Framework'—under which universities with higher teaching quality may be allowed to charge higher fees—might affect the overall number and distribution of students across higher education institutions. While, at the time of writing, the details of this scheme are not yet clear, it seems plausible that it may introduce some additional complexities when considering socio-economic inequalities in higher education access. If students are put off by higher fees, for example, then it is possible that those from poorer backgrounds may opt for cheaper courses, which—if the lower available resources also lead to lower quality provision—might reduce the chances of higher education acting as a social leveller.

Above all, while the best available evidence to date suggests that the large increase in tuition fees that took place in England in 2012 has not reduced entry to higher education, in practice, for poor students—at least for those entering soon after school to study full-time for a first degree—there is a danger that reforms to the system in future might not be so benign. (In particular, the impact of the abolition of maintenance grants due to be introduced in September 2016 remains to be assessed.) Future governments will therefore need to weigh universities' demands for higher funding against concerns about the cost to taxpayers and students of any increase in fees.

How Can We Increase University Access for Poor Students in the Long-Run?

There are clearly a number of risks posed by future changes to the higher education funding system for the future participation rates of young people from poor backgrounds. But perhaps the biggest risk posed is that socio-economic differences in attainment earlier in the school system may not fall, or may even increase. One of the most important conclusions from this book is the absolutely crucial role of prior attainment in explaining the socio-economic gaps in university access, and hence that improving the early academic achievement of poor children in primary, and particularly secondary, school is vital if the number of poor students going to university is to be substantially increased.

At least some of the schemes that are currently used to try and 'widen' participation in higher education by universities and other organizations are aimed at raising aspirations, providing information, or offering financial assistance.[1] Such schemes are predicated on the idea that students' aspirations, knowledge, or resources are lacking, rather than their prior achievement. Some of these schemes have been shown to be effective at increasing the propensity of qualified students to apply to or enter (high status) universities, but, if the major reason for lower participation by poor students is their weak prior achievement as we suggest in this book, then such activities are only likely to make a difference at the margin (unless they also have positive benefits for student achievement). To revolutionize university entry amongst those from disadvantaged backgrounds will require policies to increase their achievement earlier in the education system.

As we discussed in Chapter 6, a whole raft of policies have been implemented in recent decades by successive governments to try to narrow the socio-economic gap in achievement in schools and hence 'widen' participation in higher education. The success of these policies is reviewed elsewhere in the literature, but they have ranged from spending more money in the earliest years of a child's life, through to school reforms and attempts to improve teacher quality, and on to financial incentives to encourage pupils to stay in school beyond the school leaving age. They have produced decidedly mixed results. Better evidence is needed to understand how best to increase the school achievement of students from disadvantaged backgrounds. The work

---

[1] Such policies include bursaries, and the provision of information, advice, and guidance at various points prior to university entry, e.g. by attending a 'summer school'. We discussed some of these policies in Chapter 6.

of the Education Endowment Foundation (EEF), a charity endowed with funds by the government, is aimed at narrowing the socio-economic gap in pupil achievement in both primary and secondary schools in England. The Foundation has funded a large number of quite diverse randomized control trials, trying to test what works. While this evidence base is still emerging, it is clear that there is no silver bullet here. A wide range of different policies will be needed to reduce the socio-economic gap in achievement and having a robust evidence base on how to do this is essential.

Given the variation in returns to higher education discussed in Chapter 1, it is also vital to consider not only access to higher education in general and how it varies by socio-economic background, but how participation varies by institution and degree subject as well. We have shown that the socio-economic gaps in participation at high status universities are particularly stark. Since students who attend higher status universities go on to earn more in the labour market, the very steep socio-economic gradient in access to these institutions has major implications for social mobility. A pressing policy concern for the government is therefore not simply how to 'widen' participation in higher education generally, but to ensure greater representation of students from poorer backgrounds in the highest status institutions more specifically.

Our evidence suggests that the main reason why poorer students are less likely to attend higher status institutions is, again, that they have weaker exam results at ages 16 and 18. The best way to tackle this issue is thus very similar to the conclusions for higher education participation overall: to continue to improve the school system and help to raise the achievement levels of students from poorer backgrounds. However, GCSE and A-level subject choice also has a small but potentially important role to play here, and it is vital that students understand which subjects they need to undertake at these levels in order to study particular subjects at university and also to make their qualifications as attractive as possible to high status institutions. This is an area in which better information could be provided.

Over and above increasing the attainment and improving the subject choice of pupils from poorer backgrounds, there is more that could potentially be done to reduce the socio-economic gaps in access to high status institutions, however. This is because, in contrast to the evidence for all institutions, we cannot entirely explain the socio-economic differences in entry to high status institutions using prior attainment alone. We presented evidence that a small number of poor students who get the necessary grades to go to a high status university do not do so. Of course, this may be a rational choice for these students, but if there is a danger that some young people are not applying to high status institutions because they do not think they will get in or because they think they would not 'fit in' if accepted, then this may be another area where better advice and guidance is warranted.

What is the Role of Universities in 'Widening' Access?

Given this, what role should universities be playing in raising the university entry rates of young people from poor backgrounds? The importance of attainment earlier in the education system does not absolve universities of all responsibility, and in fact there has already been a sea change in both the resources that universities devote to widening participation, and the methods they have used to do so, since the introduction of the Office for Fair Access (OFFA) in 2012. But the evidence base underpinning these decisions is lagging behind the intention. While the importance of prior achievement suggests the need for earlier, longer-term interventions, there is a relative lack of evidence on the effectiveness of such interventions and hence a clear need for more robust evaluations of existing and new policies to inform universities of the most (cost) effective interventions to pursue.

Taking a system-wide approach to issues of widening participation may also be a sensible way to proceed. Currently universities are responsible for their own widening participation activities, although some do collaborate. However, similar initiatives are often carried out in isolation by different institutions, each working with a small number of pupils or schools trying to achieve similar objectives. There is a risk that such a piecemeal approach may duplicate resources in some areas and miss individuals in need of support in others. For example, coverage of students in urban areas, particularly London, is very high while some rural and particularly coastal areas have very little coverage at all.[2] Greater coordination of resources in this area would therefore be welcome, as long as any centralized scheme is properly evaluated so that an adequate picture can be gathered of 'what works'.

Greater central coordination may also foster more of the types of long-term sustained interventions that are likely to improve the academic

[2] The Higher Education Funding Council for England—the body responsible for distributing funds, including funds to widen participation, to universities—has produced analysis of areas with higher and lower than expected participation in higher education. See: http://www.hefce.ac.uk/analysis/yp/gaps/.

achievement of poor students. Activities that may in the long run be effective at increasing rates of entry to higher education, such as interventions focused on younger children in early secondary school, may not specifically benefit the university undertaking them. Pupils may go on to a range of institutions, not just the university that delivered the programme. This means there is some tension between what may be of most benefit to students and what may be of most benefit to universities, and universities may need to be actively incentivized to choose the strategies that will yield the greatest benefits for students. Such incentives will need to be compatible with the individual institutional targets on widening participation set with the Office for Fair Access.

Focusing on longer-term interventions to increase student attainment may help to reduce socio-economic gaps in university entry in future, but what can and should universities be doing to help increase the participation rates of young people from disadvantaged backgrounds in the short-term? Many universities are already using other strategies to try to admit more students from poorer families. Our work shows that disadvantaged students who do succeed in getting into university have lower grades, on average, than more advantaged students at the same institution studying the same subject. This is suggestive of some degree of what is known as 'contextualized admissions': universities offering applicants from more disadvantaged backgrounds marginally lower grade offers, thus making it slightly more likely that they will achieve the grades required to be admitted.

As discussed in Chapter 7, what lies behind the notion of contextualized admissions is a desire to admit applicants on the basis of their 'potential' to do well: to lower grade offers to students from some backgrounds in an attempt to equalize the performance of all groups, on average, at university.[3] Our research suggests that were universities to wish to adopt formal contextualized admission processes, they should allow for differences in the type or performance of school attended, rather than the family background or type of neighbourhood in which individuals have grown up. This is because our research shows that individuals who attend lower performing schools go on to do better at university, on average, than those who attend higher performing schools for a given level of achievement on entry, but that the same is

---

[3] This is not the same as 'affirmative action', which might mean going further and admitting students from certain backgrounds who may end up doing less well at university, on average, than students admitted via the usual route. In this way, contextualized admissions policies differ from those that have been used in other countries, such as the USA, in an attempt to reduce differences in university attendance by race, for example.

not true, on average, when comparing those from lower socio-economic backgrounds or low participation neighbourhoods. This implies that the GCSE and A-level performance of students from lower-performing schools is lower than it might otherwise have been (and that of students from higher-performing schools higher than it might otherwise have been) because of the school they attended, but that at university their true potential is evident. Many universities do already give some consideration to an individual's school when making entry offers, but a better understanding of the extent and impact of such policies is needed.

Indeed, while some universities are open about the fact that they contextualize admissions offers, and the way in which they do it, for other universities practices are less transparent. Negative media coverage has suggested that it amounts to discrimination against young people from privileged backgrounds or private schools. Universities also face mixed incentives: while meeting the targets for admitting students from poorer socio-economic backgrounds set out in their access agreements is crucial, university league tables—of which there are myriad, none prescribed by the government—often incorporate measures of 'average tariff entry'. That is, measures of the average A-level or equivalent grades of students who are admitted to a particular institution. This means that any reduction in A-level grade admissions offers may have negative consequences for positions in 'league tables'. We would strongly support moves to omit contextualized admissions offers from university league tables, as advocated by the IPPR Commission on the Future of Higher Education.[4]

Further work is needed to assess the extent of contextualized admissions going on in the university system and its impact on student entry, retention, and achievement. It may be that more active and transparent contextualized admissions policies need to be encouraged, but the full implications of doing this also need to be understood. However, given that the benefits of going to university arise from the acquisition of a degree and not just the act of going for a period of time, it is not enough for poor students to enrol in university; they must also complete their degrees successfully and hence contextualized admissions need to be done appropriately and with sufficient support for students who might otherwise struggle.

---

[4] See IPPR (2013), *A Critical Path: Securing the Future of Higher Education in England*, IPPR Commission on the Future of Higher Education.

What Can be Done to Reduce Socio-Economic Differences in Degree Outcomes?

Leaving to one side the issue of actively admitting students from disadvantaged schools, neighbourhoods, or families with lower grades than those from more advantaged environments, there is evidence that those from poorer backgrounds perform worse, on average, once they arrive at university compared with their peers from better-off backgrounds. As was the case with entry to higher education, a substantial part of the reason why is the difference in academic preparation on arrival at university, again reinforcing our conclusions about the importance of reducing socio-economic inequalities in attainment earlier in the school system in order to tackle inequalities at university as well.

But, in contrast to the results for entry, reducing differences in GCSE and A-level achievement seems unlikely to close the gaps in university outcomes. A feeling of 'belonging' seems key to encouraging students to remain in higher education, and the idea that they do not 'fit in' seems to be more common amongst those from lower socio-economic backgrounds, meaning that policies to increase retention and progression are vital to maximize the outcomes of these students as well. While there is relatively little robust quantitative evidence available on 'what works' to reduce drop-out and increase attainment at university, the existing evidence points to some relatively simple strategies that might help, including proactively contacting students at key transition points and redesigning induction events to promote peer interaction through small group work with an academic focus. The extent to which such policies benefit those students most at risk of dropping out or falling behind— and hence the extent to which they are likely to reduce socio-economic inequalities in these outcomes—is not clear, however, and more research is needed to help plug these gaps in knowledge.

Even less is known about how to reduce socio-economic inequalities in post-graduation outcomes. The introduction of a new income-contingent loan for Masters students in 2016 might help to 'widen' access to postgraduate education by overcoming the need to find money from other sources to pay (sometimes extremely high) fees upfront. But there remains a question mark over the number of recent undergraduates who will be willing to add to their already substantial undergraduate debts (or who will be able to make repayments of a further 6 per cent of income above the £21,000 threshold, concurrently with the 9 per cent repayments made towards their undergraduate loans). And with no fee regulation in the postgraduate market, it is unclear whether the scheme will reduce the upfront costs of participation or whether fees may simply increase with the introduction of this support. Future governments will need to consider the responses of individuals and universities to the change in incentives, alongside the cost of offering loans, in order to ensure that it achieves the aim of genuinely improving access to postgraduate study.

Chapter 8 also showed that there were differences in the type of job and wages earned by graduates from different backgrounds, even if they had studied the same subject at the same university and graduated with the same degree class. In particular, graduates who attended independent schools before going to university appear to go on to do better in the labour market, even if they have the same educational profile as a graduate who attended a state school. In other words, even once students have completed their higher education, those from less privileged backgrounds continue to do less well in the labour market. Higher education does not, in this sense, level the playing field. It is less clear what government intervention can do to address this problem, but it is encouraging that the government's social mobility indicators (introduced in 2013) currently include two measures relating to higher education outcomes and access to the professions, meaning that the issue is at least on the radar of policymakers. Ensuring that employers consider the nature of their hiring policies is also likely to be important for success in tackling this issue, and there might additionally be a role for universities to provide more support and career guidance for students from poor backgrounds as they move into the labour market.[5]

Final Thoughts

This book has highlighted that there are large socio-economic inequalities in access to higher education amongst young full-time students in England. These inequalities widen as a result of further socio-economic differences in outcomes during and after university, meaning that the percentage of pupils from lower socio-economic backgrounds who end up with a degree (and go on to work in a professional occupation after

---

[5] See, for example, Ashley, L. (2015), *A qualitative evaluation of non-educational barriers to the elite professions*, Report to the Social Mobility and Child Poverty Commission; Bridge Group (2016), *Socio-economic diversity in the Fast Stream*, Report to the Cabinet Office on the Civil Service Fast Stream.

graduation) is substantially lower than the percentage of pupils from higher socio-economic backgrounds who do so.

At the heart of these socio-economic inequalities in outcomes at and after higher education are inequalities in attainment earlier in the education system, especially at secondary school. Reducing these inequalities is therefore vital to transforming access to university, especially to high status institutions. This does not absolve universities of their responsibility for differential access: there is clearly an opportunity for them to work with schools and other stakeholders to help reduce these inequalities in attainment. There is also much that can be done in the meantime to ensure pupils who are already qualified to go on to higher education make the optimal choice of subject and institution for them.

And there is definitely more that universities could and should be doing to increase the retention, progression, and attainment of students from lower socio-economic backgrounds. This is not a problem that is confined to lower status institutions: it is, to an extent, common to all institutions in England, and thus needs to be tackled across the board. In particular, we need more robust quantitative evidence on 'what works' in this area, from participation through to degree achievement and post-graduation outcomes. The same rigour that is being applied to interventions designed to raise the attainment of children earlier in the school system needs to be brought to bear on interventions in higher education as well.

In conclusion, our work has clear messages for various stakeholders in higher education. In particular, we recommend that:

- Efforts to increase the participation of young people from disadvantaged backgrounds at university should focus on raising the achievement of these children in secondary schools.

- Universities should be incentivized to adopt contextualized admissions policies (which should focus on making allowance for the schools that young people attend in the first instance). This could be helped by encouraging league table producers to exclude a certain proportion of entry offers when calculating universities' average tariff entry.

- All substantive new initiatives designed to 'widen' participation, retention, and advancement in higher education should be evaluated in a robust manner. Where possible, this should include a quantitative assessment of the impact of the policy, estimated by comparing outcomes of participating students with those of a suitably chosen 'control' group of similar students who do not receive the intervention.

- Any further changes made to university funding and student support in future must continue to ensure that students do not have to make significant financial contributions upfront to the cost of their higher education.

Above all we highlight that the path to university success is a long one and at every point on that path children from more disadvantaged backgrounds need to be supported. All the actors involved have their role to play and what is crucial is that a base of suitable evidence continues to be built on which effective policies can be put in place to achieve this aim.

Name Index

Subject Index

A-level exams 8, 37, 38, 61, 80–1, 87, 104,
    115, 125
  subject choice 81–4
achievement during school *see* schools,
    attainment during school and
    university entry
administrative data *see* data
adverse selection *see* loans, adverse
    selection
affirmative action 148
Aimhigher 105–6
aspirations *see* family background,
    expectations about applying to
    university
attainment during school *see* schools
Australia 18, 43, 85–7
  income-contingent loans 31, 43

Barnett formula *see* devolution, Barnett
    formula
binary divide *see* polytechnics
British Social Attitudes survey 8, 28
Browne Review 25
bursaries *see* students, bursaries, and
    scholarships

Cambridge 5
Canada 18, 43, 85–7
charter schools *see* USA, charter schools
'contextualized' offers *see* university,
    'contextualized' offers
credit market failure 26, 86

data 4, 20
  administrative data on children in English
    schools 20, 73
  administrative data on student loans 130
  comparability across countries
    14–19, 66
  Destinations of Leavers from Higher
    Education survey 129
  Longitudinal Study of Young People in
    England 96, 103
  Student Income and Expenditure
    Survey 49

quality 20, 73, 75, 85, 128–9
UCAS 58
see also family background, measurement;
    evidence
Dearing Report 29
debt *see* 30–1, 35, 50–5
  aversion 33, 143
  credit cards 31–3, 142
  repayment *see* graduates, repayment of
    loans
  write-off 30, 52
  see also higher education, funding; loans
degree
  class *see* university, degree class; family
    background, degree class
  subject 9
  rate of return 8–9, 26–7, 80–1, 127
    family background 137–8
    degree class 133
    high status universities 9
    private 26, 29
    social 26
    see also graduates, earnings
deprivation *see* family background,
    measurement
Destinations of Leavers from Higher
    Education survey *see* data
devolution 20
  Barnett formula 41
disadvantage *see* family background,
    measurement
discount rate 53–4
drop-out *see* university, drop-out

EBacc ('English baccalaureate') 82–3
earnings *see* degree, rate of return;
    graduates, earnings
Education Endowment Foundation 146
efficiency, economic 10, 26
entry rates *see* university, entry rates; family
    background, entry to university
equity 10, 26–7
  see also social mobility
ethnicity *see* university, entry rates, ethnic
    group